THE CHAPLAIN

Luke Monahan SM and Caroline Renehan

The Chaplain:

A FAITH PRESENCE IN THE SCHOOL COMMUNITY

An Initiative of the Post-Primary Diocesan Advisers, Dublin

the columba press

First published in 1998 by
The Columba Press
55A Spruce Avenue, Stillorgan Industrial Park, Blackrock, Co Dublin

Designed by Bill Bolger
Additional illustrations by Statia Davey-Brown
Origination by The Columba Press
Printed in Ireland by Colour Books Ltd, Dublin

ISBN 1 85607 225 8

Acknowledgements

The authors and Post-Primary Diocesan Advisers, Dublin, wish to thank the following people for their kind assistance and encouragement in the production of this book: Dr Desmond Connell, Archbishop of Dublin, who granted his approval of the contents of the text prior to publication. Fr Dermot Lane who took valuable time to write the foreword and make helpful suggestions and comments along the way. Dr Andrew McGrady who painstakingly transferred data on a number of occasions to facilitate computer compatibility. Fr Paddy Greene, Fr James Norman, Sr Christina Greene, Fr Aidan Kieran, Fr Dan Joe O'Mahony, and Fr Tony Coote who originally met with the authors and Diocesan Advisers to offer their advice and ideas on chaplaincy at the outset of this project.

We also very much appreciate the work of those who contributed to the reflections located at the end of the book. In addition, we are grateful to Fr Eugene Kennedy and Fr Donal Neary for advice on matters relating to certain aspects of the text in some of its more specialised areas. Particular thanks goes to the Marist Fathers and the Marino Institute of Education who granted valuable time to Luke Monahan in the writing of the text.

Contents

Foreword

Dermot A. Lane

The White Paper on education, *Charting our Education Future* (1995), talks about the importance of every school providing pupils with an experience of pastoral care. Everybody would agree with this particular recommendation and it is only fair to acknowledge that the teaching profession in Ireland has been outstanding for the quality of pastoral care shown to pupils in the educational system. Every second family in Ireland could tell a moving tale about how the pastoral intervention of a concerned teacher helped to keep their child on the right road. The pastoral performance of teachers in Ireland is second to none.

However, one would have to be an ostrich with one's head stuck permanently in the sand to fail to notice that something quite dramatic is happening among pupils in schools in Ireland. It is extremely difficult to charter the changes taking place in schools in contemporary Ireland.

Most would agree that there are cultural changes taking place that do impact on the educational environment in which young people grow up. These cultural changes include the communications revolution: the subtle power of advertising, the pervasive influence of media and market values, and immediate access to an endless flow of information. Another cultural shift is the changing sociology of the family in Ireland: single parent families, working parents, and unemployed parents. A third cultural shift is the declining influence of political and religious institutions upon the lives of young people in Irish society. A fourth cultural change is the ever-increasing influence of the peer-group upon the behaviour, values and beliefs of those around them.

Not all cultural change should be deplored but what is disturbing is the absence of any critical analysis of the impact, positive or negative, of these changes on the educational environment of young people in schools today. Schools are expected to fill any void that may arise from these or other cultural changes. Whenever a particular problem arises within society, people inevitably turn to schools to make up for the deficits of civic and political institutions.

Recent surveys have begun to highlight serious problems arising in the lives of young people in Ireland today. For example, the European School Survey Project on Alcohol and Other Drugs, released in September 1997, reveals that Irish students are top of the league among twenty-six European countries in binge drinking, and second when it comes to taking cannabis and other illegal drugs. This particular research was carried out on 1,900 sixteen-year-old students. Another survey conducted by the Association of Secondary Teachers of Ireland (ASTI) indicates that 13% of schools surveyed had experience of student suicide. More specifically, a study entitled *Suicide – Who are the Victims?*, discussed in the *Irish Journal of Psychiatry (1997)*, suggests that suicide among young people, especially males, is on the increase and is becoming an apparent option for young people when times are bad.

It is in the context of these cultural shifts and recent survey findings that one must warmly welcome the publication of *The Chaplain: A Faith Presence in the School Community*. This text will be a most helpful resource for the whole school community: principals, teachers, counsellors, religious educators, and especially chaplains. This publication is timely, offering valuable resource material and challenging commentaries by experienced practitioners in the field of holistic pastoral care.

Chaplains in schools are key players in the delivery of education. The chaplain is seen by some simply as someone who provides a kind of ambulance service when things go wrong in the school, and of course this is important. However, the chaplain also has a positive role to play in developing the full potential of young people: physical, psychological, spiritual and religious. In addition, the chaplain has a unique role to play in co-ordinating the pastoral care provided by teachers and the different support systems on offer from the wider community. If it is true to say, and I believe it is, that young people learn to love by being loved, to trust by being trusted, to value by being valued, then chaplains have a most important role to play in effecting the holistic development of pupils.

By any standards, the work of the chaplain is not easy and all the signs of the time suggest the growing importance of the contribution the chaplain can make to good schooling. This book, *The Chaplain: A Faith Presence in the School Community*, is a most valuable contribution to the pastoral care of young people in schools in contemporary Ireland.

Mater Dei Institute, Dublin

Why Chaplains?

'*What is it you do?*' A chaplain ten years in the role was confronted with this question by an in-coming first year student, and before being able to formulate an answer a sixth year student came up behind them and declared '*Everything and nothing – the chaplain is just here with us*'.

'... here with us' is a striking part of the sixth year student's comment. Chaplaincy is about people – not structures, programmes, responsibilities or tasks. So as we reflect upon the role of chaplain in our schools, we come to learn of God's individual concern for all people. It is from this stand-point that we seek to outline a rationale for chaplaincy. Examination of this key role is vital to our understanding of the good of all in the school and in the wider faith community. Beginning with fundamentals, this first chapter will set out a rationale for the role of the school chaplain.

A Question of Values

When setting up a rationale for the role of the chaplain in schools, we begin to consider our values in respect of education. No one would be likely to engage in the business of education without reference to values, however unconsciously, since they direct our path through life. A set of values, therefore, is vital to the understanding of this handbook. Values significantly influence the consequent approaches adopted and actions taken by the chaplain working in the school community.

Rooted in Christ

One of the most basic values to be considered in Christian education is our rootedness in Christ. Christ has called all people to the fullness of life. This represents the central stance which he has taken in relation to each individual. Each one is loved and cherished to the point where he gave his life on the cross. Therefore, each one is invited out of love to follow the path of the Lord to the fullness of life. This path is one travelled in companionship with the Lord and animated by communion with others. It follows, then, that the values we continually draw upon come to us both from our Christian heritage and our participation in the sacramental life of the church. This means that each one of us is:

- precious in the eyes of God.
- worthy of the fullness of life.
- entitled to a deep and personal relationship with the Lord and membership of the church community.

Whole Person

More and more, people are coming to realise and accept that education is not merely about intellectual development. Instead, it is about a process which takes account of the emotional, physical, moral, intellectual, spiritual and religious dimensions of the person as a whole. For example, a student in a maths class cannot separate the grappling with algebra from the relationship with the teacher, nor can the student separate the spirit of the class from the culture of the school. Rather, through these interactions the student learns something about relationships, about justice, about authority … about algebra. Just as the teacher needs to be conscious of this 'whole person' impact, so does the chaplain need to take account of the person in the same manner. It is in this way that the whole person should be related to, cared for and provided with opportunities to reach the full potential of personhood. With this in mind, the chaplain takes the 'whole person approach' as one of the most significant values of ministry.

Spiritual and religious

Clearly any value that attempts to develop the whole person cannot ignore the spiritual and religious dimensions of life. In turn, these dimensions influence all other aspects of the person. If our maturing as individuals is to achieve its full potential, every level of the developmental self needs attention. Unfortunately, however, it is the spiritual and religious dimensions which are often neglected and sidelined.

Education: A Total Experience

Within the context of the whole-person approach, education, when it is properly fostered, is a total life experience which seeks to value and develop the person at every level. The chaplain, as such, is invited to reflect upon it in order to help others to see, to reflect, to inquire, to judge and to act wisely as they go about their daily lives.

Partnership

In recent years few enterprises have received greater attention in education than partnership. Without doubt, it is being recognised increasingly as something which contributes to the optimal educational experience of the school community. Partnership has its gift to offer and role to play in the educational system specifically if it takes place in a spirit of collaboration.

Nowhere is partnership more important than in the collaborative ministry of the churches and school communities. (Within that context, of course, both ordained and non-ordained ministers should have a mandate from the local ordinary to carry out their duties.)

Both of these communities have the welfare of the individual as their common goal. If a true sense of direction is to manifest itself, it will do so through dialogue. Dialogue is the key for respective responsibility, articulation of values and differing approaches. For example, in schools where the trusteeship is fully or partially the responsibility of the christian churches, the values are gospel based. However, collaboration is also required for the recognition and respect of perspectives other than those based on gospel values.

Chaplaincy is an essential component in the structure of the school. It is not an 'added extra'. For this reason the school as a whole must be involved at every level in the development and exercise of the role of the chaplain. Collaborative ministry is what chaplaincy is all about but this can only be successful if that ministry takes place within a whole school context. The ministry of chaplaincy is not a 'once off' procedure but an ongoing process.

Missioned
The role of the chaplain in collaboration with others is of great importance to the church community. The chaplain, on behalf of the church, cares for the spiritual life of those in the school. Thus, acting in a supportive and resourceful manner, the chaplain represents the faith community's concerns for all its members, especially those who wish to:
- celebrate their faith;
- deepen their faith commitment;
- explore the values of Christ as lived in the church community;
- have one who is a caring and spiritual presence among them.

Cardinal Basil Hume, addressing a conference on education in the spring of 1995, summed up a number of the points made above when he commented:

The purpose of education is to develop integrated human beings ... The task of the church in education can rarely have been more urgent or more difficult. It is also one of the most vital contributions the church can make to the renewal of our cultural and social life. (Cited in Association of Catholic Chaplains in Education, *Chaplaincy: The Change and the Challenge,* Chelmsford: Matthew James Publishing, 1996.)

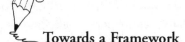

Towards a Framework

If the task of the church in education is as urgent as Basil Hume suggests, then it is timely to offer a framework for the role of the chaplain in school. While the framework will be broadly based, the following is a core statement which will serve as a point of reference throughout this handbook:

> ## The chaplain,
> ## as a faith presence,
> ## committed to the values of Christ,
> ## and on behalf of the church and school communities,
> ## accompanies each person on the journey through life.

It is important to clarify this core statement in order to focus upon consequent planning and action:

> *'faith presence'*: the chaplain is one who is animated by a close relationship with Christ. Through the strength of this relationship the chaplain, in turn, is in a position to become a *faith presence* for others. This means *being with* others and paying attention to the quality of that being with. The chaplain, as *faith presence,* is open, accepting, respecting, sharing, learning and invitatory.

'committed to the values of Christ': the chaplain recognises that the most effective way to follow Christ is in the effort to *live* the values of Christ. These values are the foundation stones that hold together the framework of school chaplaincy – not personal needs or projects. The practice of living out Christ's values daily will support and challenge the chaplain.

'on behalf of': here it is understood that the chaplain is in constant communication with the school and church communities. Their mandate is that the chaplain should be an identifiable facilitator for the spiritual welfare of students and related school personnel. This does not mean that all responsibility for spiritual welfare should rest with the chaplain, but that the chaplain is supported by, and accountable to, these communities in the exercise of the role.

'Church and school communities':

the Church community: invites all to the fullness of life through its deep personal love of Jesus Christ, through its mature knowledge, love and understanding of the faith. From this invitation stems the church's involvement with, and commitment to, education. The appointment and commissioning of a chaplain, in collaboration with the school community, is one of many responses made by the church in its pastoral mission to chaplaincy.

The school community: is concerned with the total welfare of all its members. While this includes respect for the intellectual development of the student, emphasis is also placed on the spiritual and religious aspects of the person. In schools, especially where the ethos draws upon gospel values, the chaplain has a significant part to play in supporting, encouraging and helping to formulate the ethos. (Ethos is the core value which informs the present life and future direction of the school.)

'accompanies': if there is a central gospel text for chaplains it is the Emmaus Story – *the* accompaniment story for all Christians. With this story in mind; the chaplain draws on the example of Christ as the one who meets people in their present situation, walks with them, invites them to a fuller life in Christ, acknowledges their fears/ needs/hopes, and accompanies those who have a desire to draw closer to the Lord.

'each person': exclusion of anyone is not acceptable to the chaplain. The chaplain is open to and has concern for each and every member of the school community including students, parents, academic and support staff, past-pupils and management.

'journey through life': the chaplain has the privilege of walking part of life's iourney with each individual. This is characterised by respect, support, hope and challenge.

From Why to Who

The above chapter has sought to put in place a rationale for school chaplaincy. Now it is time to move from the 'why' of chaplaincy to the 'who' of chaplaincy. Based on this working framework, we will now explore the qualities for the role and how that role might be developed.

To reflect upon

What are your educational values?

What is the shared purpose between church and school in your experience?

Answer this question for yourself – 'Why chaplaincy?'

Person for the Role

Documents which contain directions and guidelines cannot take the place of the person. They are brought to life only through the individual's life of faith, personality, and creativity. In this chapter what is avoided is the presumption that the chaplain must be a certain type of person with a specific type of nature or character. (Not everyone has the makings of a chaplain despite training or study.) Without intending presumption, this chapter attempts to offer some thoughts worthy of consideration. As you read you might ask yourself, 'Where do I fit in here?'

Looking at Qualities

There is no blueprint on the *who* of chaplaincy. Chaplains, their personalities and their natures are as varied as the personalities and natures of the people to whom they minister. Even as the chaplain sets foot in a school for the first time, the influence of many factors will change part of that chaplain's outlook forever. These factors include school climate and context, inpenetrable structures, hallowed regulations and, indeed, other personalities both strong and weak. Yet, experienced chaplains are all too aware that certain specific qualities pertinent to chaplaincy are essential for the successful implementation of the ministry.

The list of qualities proposed below will probably not come as a great surprise. Nonetheless, what is vital is the reflection that occurs around them. While considering the following list, you are invited to focus on the following two questions:

How would you prioritise the qualities for the role of chaplain?
To what extent do you possess the qualities you prioritise?

Faith Life: a personal relationship with God as expressed in the life of the church.

Commitment to the Church: an understanding and appreciation of the faith.

Personal Integration: integration of the spiritual, emotional, psychological. Awareness of self – strengths, weaknesses, values, attitudes, needs and wants. Takes responsibility for self. Has personal support structures.

Relational: able to build significant relationships with all in the school community – an ease with people of all ages, particularly youth.

Collaborative: ability to work with others, to engage with them in partnership. Contribute as a member of a team - either in a leadership or a membership role.

Leadership: to take initiative, to animate and to lead *with* people. Lead by witness. Ability to take a stand.

Openness: respectful of the values and views of others. Ability to listen and learn from others. Adaptable in the light of changing circumstances. Sensitive and observant to the needs of each member of the school community.

Justice: to be a friend to those in need, neglected, on the fringes. Seeks to safeguard the ethos of the school.

Sense of Vocation: has a clear sense of mission on behalf of the faith and school communities.

Ease with Self: a sense of humour. Relaxed with self so as to focus on the other.

Creative: seeks to initiate new ideas and strategies in response to the needs of the school community.

Awareness of the World of Education: is current with issues of importance to students, staff, parents. Awareness of significant trends in education.

Ideal and Real

Even though the above list is not exhaustive, few people will possess all of these qualities. Clearly, the quality chart is necessarily idealistic but it provides a number of 'indicators' when evaluating the role of chaplain. Note the term 'indicators' is used, not 'qualifications'. The business of qualifications, that is skills and training, is a separate matter. Here, instead, we are focusing on the *person,* the most important resource in the ministry of chaplaincy. Within that context it is appropriate to set high standards for those who would undertake the position.

Relationships: The Key

Central to understanding the role of the chaplain is to see it as relational. The two companions on the road to Emmaus were joined by the Lord and entered into relationship with him. In the same way, the chaplain enters into a whole series of relationships in order to act as a *faith presence* in the school community. The diagram opposite attempts to display this reality in graphic form. Reflect on the diagram using the prompting questions set out below:

> *What are the priority relationships in your situation?*
> *Are there relationships you neglect – do you know why?*
> *Which are the most life-giving?*
> *What is your style of relating to each?*

Students

Staff

Families

Local Parish

Religion Teachers

Pastoral Team

The Chaplain

Principal

Guidance Counsellor

Home-School Liaison

Past Pupils

Social Services

Management/Trustees

Education Secretariat
CORI
Chaplains Association

Self and
Faith Life

Network of Relationships

It is in and through an understanding of this network of relationships that the chaplain comes to terms with his/her suitability for the role. From this perspective the core statement outlined earlier now makes greater sense:

The chaplain,
as a faith presence,
committed to the values of Christ,
and on behalf of the church and school communities,
accompanies each person on the journey through life.

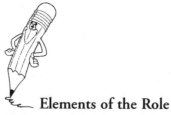 Elements of the Role

Within the context of the network of relationships and the core statement, consider some of the more pertinent elements of the ministry. The chaplain, for example:

* animates the spiritual life of the school community.
* supports the religion faculty of the school.
* facilitates the celebration of the Eucharist and the Sacrament of Reconciliation.
* provides individual/group accompaniment and spiritual guidance.
* is concerned with the articulation and implementation of the school's ethos.
* contributes to the school's pastoral team.
* assists those involved with students and/or families in difficulties.
* is a resource and spiritual support to the staff.
* provides opportunities for the spiritual welfare of families.
* maintains a close link with the local church community.
* facilitates the provision of retreats for students and also, where feasible, parents and staff.

This chapter has dealt with three essential areas in understanding the chaplain as *person* for the role: the qualities, the network of relationships involved and some key elements of chaplaincy. These will serve our exploration of the role of the chaplain in the following pages.

To reflect upon

Which of your own characteristics requires further reflection?
How clear is your school community on your role with respect to the network of relationships?
What steps can be taken to develop a whole-school approach to chaplaincy?

Exercising the Role

Being clear on values and roles with respect to chaplaincy is one thing, but *doing* something about it is quite another. Since a foundation has now been prepared, the *how* of chaplaincy requires investigation. This presupposes questions such as: how can I be with students, staff and parents in a worthwhile way?, how do I use my time?, how will I contribute to a school assembly or organise a liturgy? Different chaplains will approach these concerns in accordance with their own personalities and natures. The remainder of this handbook will provide suggestions, guidelines, ideas and resources.

Loitering with Intent

At this juncture it is important to highlight one of the great traps of school life – the tyranny of 'doing'. So easily do we get caught up in running programmes, organising events and leading groups, that we forget the importance of just spending time with people. This is not an invitation to drink coffee for the duration of our careers! Rather, it is to be conscious of the important balance between 'doing' and 'being'. Mary McKeone captures the point well in her provocatively entitled book, *Wasting Time in School,* when she writes:

> *Part of our ministerial gift is time and we 'waste' it well by being prepared*

to give it away lavishly … ensuring that it is quality time we give away, and not the last tatters of a twenty-hour scrum. (M. McKeone, *Wasting Time in School*, Middlegreen: St. Paul's, 1993.)

Again we are brought back to the Emmaus story: the Lord gave time to be with his companions, to listen to them, to allow them to know him and open up to him. Chaplaincy in this respect can often be very difficult in a strictly timetabled environment such as school life. Nonetheless, it is an essential and valuable practice for the chaplain to work around this sometimes frustrating limitation.

Available

At all times, particularly in the early stages of being in a new school, a chaplain needs to spend time being available. It is necessary to greet people in the corridor, walk around the school yard, chat in the staffroom, and become a presence that says, 'I'm available if you want to talk.' Contrast this with rushing from place to place and appearing only when absolutely necessary. Once again, we should remind ourselves of the core guiding statement outlined in the first and second chapters, i.e. chaplaincy is primarily about being a *faith presence.*

With Students

Each chaplain finds a unique and special way of relating to young people … there is no best way. The motivation for relating to the students comes from a belief, on the part of the chaplain, that faith can be nurtured primarily through witness and support. Spending time in a way that is authentic and communicates availability to students is vital. For example, if you are utterly disinterested in sport, don't suddenly become a collector of player cards – your lack of passion will shine through! Nor might the finer points of Swahili grammar be the place to start! Rather, use your own interests as the basis for communication. Your common sense will dictate the path you should follow in this area. Consider, for example, computers, music, TV programmes, sport and other such pastimes.

Some Suggestions

Getting to Know You

Visit each class at the beginning of the year for ten minutes. Have a piece prepared so that your visit has a clear purpose. For example:

* what is the need for a chaplain?
* what you do.
* events with which you are involved.
* reasons students might avail of the chaplain.
* when and where you are available.

Present this in an interesting way – on a chart, a handout, a diagram.

Special Interest Groups

Getting to know students is particularly valuable in a small group context. Young people value being part of groups for a sense of belonging, friendship and purpose. Here the choice of group will be helped by considering the following criteria:

* is there an indentifiable need among students for this group?
* will the group service a gap in the school's present provision?
* it is not just your personal hobby-horse.
* have you an interest in the group's cause/purpose?
* the group will have a future independent of you.

Examples of such groups are:

guitar and music group, justice and peace, Vincent de Paul, gospel meditation, cycling, school radio, students' newsletter, guided reading …

Working with staff

The teaching staff in so many ways carry the life of the school. If we want to check the operational – *the living* – values of a school, it is the staff who will be our key point of reference. They are the central implementers of ethos in the day to day interactions of the school. Therefore, it is crucial that the chaplain should be a *presence* among staff. It is important not to presume on their needs or take for granted that the support offered is the correct one on the part of the chaplain. Instead, spend time listening, pick up hints and vibes, and be pre-emptive and tentative to any suggestions that might be made. Chaplains often worry about whether or not teachers see them as having a 'soft' job. The clarifying of your role with staff is essential, not just at the outset of your appointment but regularly, throughout your time with the school community.

Many strands

Your colleagues on the staff will have many and various values, beliefs and views in respect of the church and God. Engaging with people from different beliefs can bring an experience which ranges anywhere from being burdensome to being an opportunity for mutual growth and learning. Universal acceptance on these matters is not to be expected in every staffroom. An array of responses to you as chaplain may come in the form of welcome, suspicion, indifference, respect, resentment and warmth. Entering such a situation can be a daunting prospect. For these reasons your own faith and personal integration are very important. The following suggestions may contain many obvious ideas as to how you might mingle and, through your ministry, build up a good working relationship:

Some Suggestions

a. Support religion faculty

This group is central for the chaplain. Support the religious education co-ordinator and avoid leading the team, unless that is part of your brief. Offer support by helping to find resource materials, ideas, plan liturgies, retreats, special week of religious activities, programme content. Seek their support for your role.

b. Facilitate a special liturgy for past and present members of staff

Many staff are delighted when an initiative is taken to recall past staff members and their families. It could take the form of a simple Eucharist or short prayer service at a time when all who wish to attend can do so. A cup of tea afterwards adds to the experience.

c. Join staff social committee

Assisting the staff to relax is not only beneficial for teachers but also adds to the overall climate of school. Many staffs are seeing the value of being together in a relaxed way rather than just being in the pubs or on the golf course! Some possibilities: theatre nights, table quiz, bowling, hiking.

d. Attend staff meetings

The chaplain – particularly fulltime – will be greatly assisted in under-standing staff issues by participating in these meetings. While the chap-lain does not have a partisan or disciplinary role, a contribution can be made from a distinct perspective. Areas of specific concern to the chap-lain will be the ethos of the school, the welfare of staff, parents and stud-ents, the religion team, and the spiritual life of the school community.

e. Organise an evening of reflection for staff

One optional event is where staff might be invited to an evening of reflection and relaxation. Invite a speaker to address a topic of concern, e.g. stress, bereavement, teen culture, drugs, prayer and meditation. Then perhaps some quiet time, with a liturgy or prayer service, and fin-ish with a light supper – preferably in a convenient location away from the school.

f. Membership of pastoral team

This key group of people will probably want your support in whatever way you can offer it. With the group, discern how best you might be of service *re* the needs of the school, the competencies of group members, your skills and availability. This could mean presence at meetings, facili-tating specific topics with students or teachers, contacting outside speak-ers and specific social and community groups.

g. Contribute resources: books. videos worksheets

Many teachers are grateful for resources and insights into new approach-es and methodologies. Even though these may be outside your area of expertise, the chaplain is often well placed to come across material that might be of use to others who do not teach religion. Keep an eye open and pass the material on if it comes your way.

Supporting parents

The chaplain has a care for all members of the school community. Parents in particular can be offered much needed support by the presence of a chaplain. The value of partnership has been highlighted in recent times especially with regard to parents. It is appropriate that parents are given the opportunity to contribute to the life of the school, particularly with respect to the ethos, policy and programmes. However, at times many parents are reluctant to become involved. Some possible reasons might be:

* a real or perceived lack of welcome.
* home or work commitments.
* poor experience in their own education.

It is incumbent on the school, of which the chaplain is an integral part, to encourage involvement in a range of activities. Parents then, in their own inimitable way, will be better able to shape and support the work of the chaplain.

Building links

As a homogenous group, parents do not exist. They are all different with their own life story to tell. No single response meets the needs of all. The chaplain listens and discerns before taking initiatives. Assistance often comes in the form of the home-school liaison co-ordinator which some schools are fortunate to have on their staff. The ability to link with this service would be invaluable to the chaplain. In schools where this resource is unavailable other means will need to be employed such as making the connection with the local parish, setting up a parent resource group, joining a special staff/parent committee.

Some Suggestions

a. Parent Resource Group

In liaison with the school's Parents' Council it may be helpful to gather a group of parents who are interested in becoming a focus group for parent support. With this group, decide what form the support should take: parenting courses, assistance with student retreats, involvement in senior religion, speakers on topics of interest. This group can be of support to you and a fund of ideas and resources for the whole school community.

b. Chaplain's Newsletter

A further point of contact can be either a chaplain's 'corner' in the regular school newsletter or a special edition a couple of times a year, with notices, reflective passages, information on role, events, availability. An innovative format is suggested – student computer wizards will assist!

c. Twilight Retreat

A short three or four hour evening of reflection for families/parents. This may not be a year one event but perhaps in time. Prepare with parents; some input, some quiet prayer and reflection, opportunity for the Sacrament of Reconciliation and Eucharist.

d. Parent Room

If possible, provide a space for parents to call their own in the school where tea, coffee and chats can take place. This would encourage parents to become more involved with the school. Allied to this might be a special parent notice-board displaying photographs of home-school activities. In fact, photographs are a tremendous connecting feature for students and staff also.

e. Parent-Teacher Meetings

Depending on your style, be present by chatting to parents. Have a desk so that parents can pop over to you. Offer material or a brochure which describes your work and role, and possibly make a presentation to the assembly of parents. Also remember to have a care for staff who might find these meetings stressful.

f. Home Visitation

The 'how' of visitation is very much a personal matter. Whatever the chosen method, it is an invaluable service to provide. Here, you are with families on their own ground. Often this frees the conversation and allows real needs to surface. Some chaplains visit by themselves, others visit in pairs (perhaps another parent), still others have a team of 'visitors'. Another method is to have 'street meetings' where one parent hosts school-attached parents in their immediate vicinity.

g. Invitation to School Events

So many good things happen in the daily life of school which parents never hear of. Opportunities may arise where parents might be invited to school assemblies, to a particular section of a school retreat, or to fund raising events.

h. Special Liturgies

Liturgy is especially relevant at transition stages in our lives. The beginning of secondary school is an apt time to celebrate the hope of a new community coming together. Also, graduation at the end of school is a significant moment worthy of full and thoughtful liturgy. In addition, families can be invited to Advent and Lenten Services, to November remembrance liturgies, to the school's saint's day celebrations.

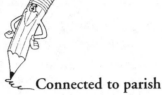

Connected to parish

All too often, unfortunately, the relationship between young people and parish is tenuous. In order that students might see possibilities for parish involvement, it is important to establish close links between the school and the parish. At this stage it might be useful to recall that the chaplain works 'on behalf of the church and school communities'. This statement implies partnership between the church and the school, with the chaplain as the main mediator. A key part of the ministry, then, is to set up relationships which will provide mutual encouragement and sustenance for all those who are courageous enough to embark on this journey. It might be useful to note that some measure of success has been achieved between primary schools and parish. The challenge now remains for those chaplains working in second level. Perhaps, therefore, the following suggestions are worthy of consideration.

Some Suggestions

a. Open Forum of Parish Personnel

As part of the religion programme, invite the clergy and other parish personnel from the locality to visit a class or year group. Have a prepared format for the occasion and some guiding questions for the visitors to use in preparing whatever input they may offer. Ask a student to introduce/thank the personnel from their parish. Have a display of photographs, parish newsletters, lists of organisations and facilities.

b. Visit of a Local Bishop

Apart from other occasions, the bishop may find it particularly worthwhile to visit the first year students, many of whom he will have confirmed. Also the sixth year students may benefit from time spent with the bishop. In order to encourage participation, students might prepare questions in advance of a visit. A carefully prepared format can lead to a most productive and enjoyable event.

c. Parish and Diocesan Offices

Very often the many and various groups, associations, organisations and services connected to the parish and diocese are unknown to students and their families. It may be useful to arrange a project in Transition Year to encourage students to research these services and arrange a presentation. Also members of these organisations may be happy to come to the school and speak to students/staff/parents.

d. Use of Parish Church Facilities

The local church is a great resource for special prayer services, retreats and catechesis. Visits familiarise students with the building and its significant parts. They also provide an opportunity for the local parish personnel to meet the students.

e. Parish Events

Representation of the school through parents, students or staff at important parish events is a worthwhile experience for those involved. This may take many forms: participation in liturgy, music, artwork, readings, processions, assistance at parish social events, stewarding, entertainment, organising, membership of appropriate parish committees, youth, care for elderly, faith development.

f. Parish Fund Raising

Many fund raising events occur in schools. It would value the parish and school relationship if at least one of these events were to be centred on a parish/local need. This affords all concerned to become involved at every stage of the process.

This chapter has made an effort to unpack the *who* of chaplaincy. We recognise the great wealth of experience in our Irish context in this matter. The above represents merely a small percentage of that wealth.

To reflect upon

How can you usefully 'waste time' in school?
How can you determine the needs of the school community?
How might you facilitate school, parish, home links?

A Year in the Life

READY – AIM – FIRE: So often in ministry these actions are carried out in the wrong order – Fire, Aim, Ready. We act before we have prepared ourselves or have listened sufficiently to the needs of the community among whom we are ministering. Careful planning is essential in the work of the chaplain. This chapter will examine a possible approach to a year-long plan for school chaplaincy.

'Where do I start?'

The range of possibilities in chaplaincy is so wide and varied that it requires time and planning. Remember, however, that only so much can be done in any given year. It is best to focus energy on specific areas and build from year to year rather than try to cover every eventuality immediately. Attempting to be all things to all people is a recipe for frustration. McKeone puts this point well:

> The Chinese proverb: 'Paths are made by those who walk on them' is nowhere truer than in the ministry of a chaplain ... the work is vast and can never be completed but one small step after watching, listening, waiting may be the first in an important journey. (*Wasting Time in School*, p. 22.)

Back to School

Just as retailers are well prepared in advance of the beginning of the school term, so can the chaplain be ready in advance of the first day back. Anyone involved in school knows the all-consuming nature of the work once the year commences. If any degree of success is to be met, it is important to begin planning towards the end of the previous academic year in time for the following September. Proper planning does not have to consist of a rigid programme but some time and energy spent on the more immediate issues will pay dividends as the year progresses. Forward planning for the forseeable future will allow time and space for the unforseeable future.

Year to year

The key to success is to select and target a *limited* number of areas that might need to be addressed as the year pans out. This will ensure that those areas selected will benefit significantly from the concentrated effort. Not everything has to be accomplished in the nine months of the school year, so do not worry when more pressing issues take time from your original plan. Each school chaplain makes choices based on a reflective process of discernment. As the chaplain begins to collaborate with others, it will become evident that the priority for one chaplain is different from that of another. Some schools, for example, may require support in building up the religion department, some may wish to focus on staff morale, and others may need help in finding a space for an oratory. Whatever the choice, remember that the needs of the school community should always come before the personal aspirations of the chaplain.

Know your limits

Although needs must be identified and addressed, it would be irresponsible to rush headlong into action if you are not fully equipped to do so. Part of avoiding such a difficulty is to be aware of your own abilities and limitations. Seek assistance if, where and when it is required. Particularly in the area of spiritual guidance and counselling, the chaplain should be aware when and where to seek further assistance. Where the chaplain has something to contribute it is necessary to be clear about what is possible and what is not, what is appropriate and what is not.

Some Suggestions

Planning priorities for the year

1. Possibilities: list, with your support team if possible, all the needs of the school community perhaps in 'brainstorm' fashion. For example; school atmosphere, ethos, staff morale, parent involvement, role clarification of key personnel, discipline, spiritual dimension of school, religion faculty ...

2. Prioritise: prioritise these needs, perhaps linking needs of a similar nature. Here the views of others are essential. This exercise should be built on a long process of reflective listening.

3. Chaplain's Role: which of these priorities would benefit from your input as chaplain? It is important to be specific about what is and what is not possible.

4. Decision: which of the above prioritised needs will you decide to address in the coming year? You can only do so much ...

5. Action: how can you address this need?
* what can you do?
* when will you do it?
* what do you need in order to accomplish your goal?
* how will you evaluate what you have done?

A Year in Focus

The following is an outline of a range of possibilities which the chaplain might become involved in throughout the school year. They provide a means to explore some of the richness of chaplaincy already being experienced in our schools. Begin, perhaps, by integrating these ideas into your own school and ask yourself how they might be adapted or reworked. Further suggestions are contained in the resource ideas towards the end of the book.

Beginnings

Recall your first day at secondary school. Pemember that it is a very significant day. So many new routines are there for students to become accustomed to: a variety of teachers, a different building, new classmates, whether or not they will complete a five or a six year cycle ... While all types of preparations will have been made in advance of the incoming first-years, for example, open nights, orientation days and parent/student visits to the school, the day itself can be traumatic. The chaplain's presence, therefore, is of great support to all concerned. Consider particularly the necessity for:

- greeting students and parents as they arrive and are waiting around.
- giving a brief input to the opening assembly.
- showing students/parents around the building.
- meeting new teachers/ancillary staff.

The object of the exercise here, specifically, is to be a welcoming presence on a very significant day in the lives of students.

Building on beginnings

It was mentioned earlier that a visit to classes might be an important way to alert people to the chaplaincy role. Particular attention needs to be given to first-year students in an effort to encourage a sense of belonging to the community of the school. Indeed, religious education syllabi often have the themes of 'community and belonging' as part of their first-year programme. The chaplain could greatly contribute to these themes by facilitating an opening liturgy for first-year students, their families and their teachers. The importance of a good liturgical experience cannot be overstated, especially when it takes place during the significant transition points in our lives. The beginning of secondary school life is one such obvious occasion. Within the context of a 'faith gathering', many members of the school community often find liturgical services to be a most positive and encouraging practice.

An Opening Liturgy with First Year

Theme:
'Building Community'

There are endless possibilities – the chaplain supports and resources the religion staff and others involved.

Who to Involve
The religion teachers will be at the centre of the preparation. Nonetheless, others have a role to play such as: class tutors, the year head, home-school liaison personnel, art and music teachers. Gather the team well in advance of the liturgy itself. This affords time to make the most of the event. Perhaps the chaplain could host the first meeting over a light meal so that the sense of community being celebrated is mirrored in the group taking responsibility for the occasion.

Form of Liturgy
Having decided on a Eucharistic or other liturgical celebration, it is important to focus on how best to express the theme of community. The following are some ideas from a vast range of possibilities:

– the students design a card inviting parents and teachers to the liturgy.

– each class in first year takes a section of the liturgy.

– have all students copy their hand imprints on to a sheet of paper to decorate the altar.

– each class prepares a 'Class Shield' containing images of their identity as a group.

– students introduce sections of the liturgy, explaining the meaning of the different elements.

– link in the sacrament of Confirmation as many will have recently received this sacrament.

– invite some parents and teachers to participate by reading prayers and distributing Communion.

– music is an essential ingredient. Check with the music teacher about the school choir to form a group of first years, or invite the local folk group if this is acceptable.

– invite and involve local parish clergy and personnel.

– prepare a special prayer card for students to hand to their parents at some stage of the liturgy.

– involve students from other year groups:
> * choir for the liturgy.
> * as greeters to those attending.
> * assisting with the refreshments.
> * senior students with responsibilities for first years might be recognised formally at some stage in the liturgy.

– incorporate the ethos statement of the school into the liturgy:
> * have it especially drawn and displayed for the event.
> * students act out their interpretation of the school's ethos.
> * put the statement on one side of a prayer card.
> * a teacher, parent and student light a candle symbolising commitment to the implementation of the school's ethos.

– conclude with some refreshments for all.

Remember to keep a record of the event with a video or photographs. These will be invaluable for the graduation at the end of the students' time in school, and also as a stimulus for discussing the meaning of liturgy in religion class.

October and the Missions

The relationship between the local and the universal church is crucial. The chaplain may use the annual opportunity in October to recognise the work of the church in the mission areas of the world. The more experiential the strategy the better is the outcome. A range of events could be organised to suit the different ages concerned. Consider the following:

* a talk from a missionary home on holidays.
* a fund-raising event for a particular mission. Feedback reports might be possible.
* build up a long-term relationship with one school or parish.
* lay missionaries might discuss their experience with students/staff/parents.
* if special links exist between the local parishes and any missionary activity, a presentation might be made.

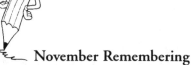

November Remembering

Remembering those who have gone before us has long been a treasured tradition. It provides us with an important opportunity to exercise our faith in God's love and mercy. See chapter 9 for a sample prayer service.

Some Suggestions

A Eucharist in Memory

Sometime in November, have a special Eucharist where all are invited to attend, perhaps just before school or at a lunchtime. Visit all the classes with a prepared sheet of paper encouraging all those who are interested to write down the names of anyone they would like to have remembered in the Eucharist. These names should then be deposited immediately into a box. Leave some spare sheets of the prepared paper with the teacher for those who are not present.

The Eucharist itself can be quite simple, perhaps with some background music as people gather and reflect.

Cemetery Care

Some students could be encouraged to assist with the cleaning up of graves. A prayer service at each cemetery might be held as a means of remembering the dead.

Visit to churches

Perhaps with junior classes it might be possible to visit local churches. Prepare a worksheet for completion by each student, for example:
  - to whom is the church dedicated?
  - name three statues located in the church.
  - what is the most attractive feature of the church?
  - sketch out the sanctuary including the altar, ambo, tabernacle ...

Advent Waiting

The season of Advent provides many opportunities for the chaplain to fulfil an important role in the school. Most schools have a number of activities running annually at this time so these can be supported and built upon. A selection of possibilities is outlined below.

Reconciliation Service

It is worthwhile building up a number of formats for use with this sacrament. Reconciliation services prepared with care can be of great value to the students. Depending on the availability of clergy, reconciliation services can take place either class by class or in year groups over a number of weeks. It is particularly helpful to give a short input before students avail of the sacrament. This input should attempt to:

- encourage reflection prior to confession.
- present a positive image of the mercy of God.
- demonstrate the relevance of the sacrament.

Reconciliation services focussing on honesty are regarded by many chaplains as a positive and most effective challenge in the lives of the students. An Examination of Conscience handout is outlined in chapter 9. Once the students complete this sheet, they might be asked to present it to the priest in order to discuss the items of significance to them. Perhaps a more in-depth discussion of some of the topics might take place in class at a later stage.

Fund-raising

Being actively involved in Christian service is undoubtedly the most effective means of reaching out to those in need. Not only does it assist the marginalised but it also helps us to understand better our calling as Christians. Rather than merely discussing the various needs of the marginalised in society we should encourage action. Students generally respond with vigour and commitment to fund-raising. It is important, therefore, to involve them as much as possible in the organisation so that they will learn from the experience. The adults concerned need to support and resource without dominating and directing. While it is often difficult to obtain a balance in this regard, it is worth the effort. Choices of charities are limitless but it may be worthwhile considering some link with local parishes. The work of the St Vincent de Paul Society, for example, is an obvious candidate for support during this Advent time.

Advent decorations

The school environment can significantly contribute to its atmosphere. While, on the one hand, dull empty walls are unlikely to encourage a sense of belonging and commitment, on the other hand, tastefully decorated spaces are more conducive to the building of community. Use of the school environment, to highlight key church seasons, is a helpful means of positive and enjoyable catechesis. Some ideas borrowed from schools around the country, such as the following, might be adapted to suit your situation:

- sponsor an Advent poster competition.
- a school Jesse Tree.
- a giant Advent calender.
- statues/posters of the main Advent characters.
- Advent 'Graffiti Wall' – with Advent phrases and drawings.
- a school crib.

Carol Service

Carol Services are featured in many schools during this period. In some, it is an event for parents and past pupils, in others, it is the end of term assembly. A careful mixture of carols, scripture readings and reflections can make these events most memorable. It is worth considering the addition of other elements such as:

- Advent posters.
- class prayers.
- student recognition in various areas of school life.
- a reflection given by one of the staff.
- symbols of fund-raising carried on during Advent.

Lenten Preparation

The season of Lent provides many opportunities to engage the school community in various activities. As with other dimensions of the chaplain's work, careful discernment is needed in choosing strategies. Attention should be given to the core meaning of the season as a preparation for the Easter event. It can be too easy for the season to turn into a merely social awareness experience. Remember that the role of the chaplain is to provide a means whereby members of the school community can integrate faith and life. Therefore, if a daily school Eucharist or prayer service takes place during Lent, efforts should be made to integrate these acts of worship into the life of the school.

Ash Wednesday

Ash Wednesday is a potent reminder of the season of Lent. Preparation is the key to making the most of the symbolism of this day. Such themes as preparation, sacrifice and charity among others should be incorporated into creative prayer services. In turn, these will encourage the students to reflect on the relevance of Lent for their lives. Various ways should be found to invite students to make a commitment for the season. They should also be encouraged to support each other in keeping to that commitment.

Daily Eucharist/Prayer Service

Advertise the daily liturgy with enthusiasm and creativity by including the use of creative posters and announcements. Prepare the oratory/liturgy space with care by considering the effect of lighting, reflective music, reading material and furnishings. With the support of the religion teachers, have each class take responsibility for the liturgy on a rota basis. The preparation may be as simple as:

- a class prayer/reflection.
- one hymn/piece of music.
- reader/server.
- greeter and oratory set-up.

Encourage staff and parents to attend. Some staff and/or parents may wish to take their turn in being responsible for the liturgy.

Faith and Justice Week

The idea here is to choose one week of Lent to focus the entire school community on faith and justice issues. A range of events can be organised to dovetail with the season and to meet the needs of each group in the school. In many schools this has become an annual event.

Some Suggestions

Faith and Justice Week

Daily Theme: each day has a theme, e.g. justice and the individual; faith and justice in our area. A series of worksheets can be prepared which are suitable for each age group. Teachers are invited to bring these to class. A prayer adapted to each day's theme is prepared.

Prayer: a prayer service for each class around central themes of the week might he conducted. Gospel meditations could be used to integrate the spiritual and the human concerns of this special week. Over time a range of prayer service styles can be developed which are best suited to the different age sroups.

Speakers: a range of speakers on various topics would be a useful resource. Many schools have built up a bank of speakers so that repetition is avoided.

Fund-raising: fund-raising competitions not only raise money but they also contribute to improving the overall climate of the school. Some examples gleaned from around the country are:

* teachers supply pictures of themselves as children – students must pay to guess who is who; match the handwriting to the teacher; teachers's sayings; match hair to eyes.
* table quiz – teams include one student from each year while a students' council sets and marks questions; offer spot prizes for the winners.
* breaktime music – during morning/lunch breaks; on one or more days of the week have a 'school radio' with songs selected by the students playing in the school yard.

Events for Parents: if you are having a Third World craft sale, advertise it in a newsletter or other medium to inform the parents who may wish to call in to the school. Also invite them to some of the speaker presentations where possible. Encourage parents to become involved in the fundraising.

Daily Newsletter: to build a sense of community prepare a one page in-house daily newsletter with the events of the day and some reflective points.

Parish Link-up Week

Lent is a very active time in the parish. Therefore, it is an ideal time for students to experience the life of their parish. One approach might be to have a different parish-linked event for each year group, for example:

First Year: hold Stations of the Cross in the local parish church.

Second Year: have the Lenten reconciliation service in the parish church, with the assistance of the local clergy and parish personnel.

Third Year: outline a project to design a section of the Holy Week church decor.

Fourth Year: the transition year students attend/assist with various prayer services in the local primary school.

Fifth Year: have a presentation by parish personnel to the students on the various groups and social services in the parish.

Sixth Year: the students might carry out a fund-raising event for a parish related charity like St. Vincent de Paul. The final presentation of the cheque should take place during a short prayer service in the parish church.

Final Term

All too quickly, the last term of the school year arrives. The chaplain is aware that the outgoing academic year must be reviewed while the incoming one requires some preliminary forward planning.

Review and Plan

Few tasks are as important as taking time to evaluate the outgoing academic year and the commencement of planning for the incoming one. Evaluation and accountability are essential at this stage, not only to oneself and to the school community, but also to God. If the Chaplain is a *faith presence* on behalf of the church and school communities, these considerations must not be overlooked. Sparsity of time in the final term, then, is no excuse for neglecting a plan of action. In addition, a tremendous benefit will accrue if this planning takes place in collaboration with the religion team, the counsellor, the home-school liaison person and the principal. Nonetheless, be sensitive to the fact that teachers in particular are under considerable pressure at this time with house and State examinations. Also, of course, it is essential to be aware that the principal's work will extend well into the summer holidays. Be patient and understanding!

Some Suggestions

Personal Review.

* what was the most worthwhile experience of the year ... for myself ... for the students ... for others in the school?
* what was the most significant spiritual occasion of the year?
* how was I most a faith presence ... do I know why?
* where did I find it most difficult to be a faith presence ... do I know why?
* what did I learn about my own faith?
* what do I most hope for in the coming year?

Evaluation of Role – where possible involve others.

* what level of clarity concerning the role of chaplain exists in the different sections of the school community?
* in reviewing the aims set out at the beginning of the year, how have they been achieved?
* in what area has there been the greatest progress?
* what are the needs that have not been met in this past year?
* what should be changed?

Planning

See again the suggested procedure at the beginning of this chapter.

The above procedure for the academic year, remember, is not carved in stone. The chaplain decides what is possible in terms of time, resources, skills and school needs. If the chaplain is to avoid frustration by being 'all things to all people', a process of discernment is the answer.

To reflect upon

Does your school regularly review and plan?

How will you discern the central aims for your role as chaplain?

What practical strategies will you put in place to achieve these aims?

Supporting the Chaplain

Clearly, a vast array of activities such as the above overstretches the abilities of any one person. For this reason, it is important to realise that the chaplain is entitled to expect support from structures already in existence. Exploration of these structures, and how they might be of assistance to the chaplain, will be examined in this chapter.

Support Structures

The chaplain is not self-sufficient, so it is vital that support structures are availed of in the development of the ministry. The primary structures which the chaplain should be aware of are those within the school community itself, those at parish/diocesan/religious level, chaplains' associations, and chaplaincy training programmes. These are a clear sign of the significance attributed to the place of chaplaincy in our schools. While some have not always been as successful as one might have hoped, nonetheless, goodwill and dedication often abound. Undoubtedly a new age is dawning in education. The ever-ready chaplain is in a strategic position to utilise these structures in the interests of the ministry. Let us consider the following four already mentioned:

* in-school community.   * parish/diocesean/religious.
* chaplains' association groups.   * training of chaplains.

In-School Community

It can be very easy for the various members of the school community to call upon the resources of the chaplain without recognising responsibility as something which should be reciprocal. Care for the chaplain is as vital as it is for any other person in the life of the school. Unlike other members of the school, however, the chaplain is *always* imaged as the one who does the supporting. For this reason it is likely that, if the chaplain does not take the initiative for self support, no one else is likely to do so either. Strange as it may seem, the chaplain must enable others to facilitate the ministry within the school community to ensure that support of the chaplain is offered on an ongoing basis. Fortunately an openness exists in most schools which automatically offers an opportunity for team membership. Generally these *in-school* structures would include the religion faculty, the pastoral team, the parent resource group and the staff social committee. Great support is also usually offered by a chaplaincy team (if one is *in-situ*), the principal, and the guidance counsellor.

Chaplaincy team

In some contexts it may be possible to have a specific chaplaincy team who share the work load. Sometimes this may require a number of chaplains for various sections of the school community. Also the participation of parents/teachers/parish personnel is vital. They should all meet regularly with the chaplain in order to evaluate the school's experience of chaplaincy, share faith and plan future strategies.

The Principal

The school principal is a central figure in the life of the school. Few would make a greater contribution to the school climate than this key figure. Therefore, it is imperative that the chaplain has a clear line of communication to the principal. Certainly, it is the duty of the chaplain to dialogue with the principal in the drawing up of the role definition for chaplaincy. Only through clarity of role and an understanding of consequent responsibilities, will the relationship between the principal and the chaplain become a fruitful one. It is worth noting that the role of principal is often lonely and demanding. So while the chaplain seeks support from the principal, there should be an awareness of the importance of being a supportive presence to the principal.

The Counsellor

The guidance counsellor carries out a very important and multi-dimensional role in the school. Since guidance counselling and chaplaincy share many areas of common concern, support for the chaplain will be forthcoming. A wise chaplain would be aware of these common concerns, as well, of course, as the radical differences in the nature of both roles. Sensitivity on the part of the chaplain, in particular, will ensure the existence of a beneficial relationship between the two parties.

Parish/Diocesan/Religious

Moving beyond the confines of the school environment, a chaplain has the right to expect support from the local parishes and from the diocese. Structures obtain in all schools whereby the local parish, the diocese and/or the religious trustees have a formal relationship with the school. The lines of communication are always open. If this is not the case, the chaplain must sensitively enquire why it is so and what action can be taken to improve relationships. In order to maintain or build up the relationship within these structures the chaplain might consider the following:

Parish

The chaplain would benefit greatly from a regular meeting with parish personnel – both clergy and those concerned with youth in the parish. This meeting might focus on such issues as:
* parish-based faith development programmes for youth.
* liturgy and the involvement of young people in the parish.
* social needs of the parish and the connection with the school community.
* sharing the ministry of working with youth.

Diocese/Religious

The support structure here might take the following form:
* in-service training for chaplains which relates directly or indirectly to their work in schools.
* availability/provision of resources.
* regular two-way communication.
* policy guidelines and practical strategic support in areas such as spiritual guidance, relationships and sexuality education.
* review and planning of the role of chaplaincy at local and regional level.
* facilitate gatherings of chaplains in cluster support groups.
* specific support regarding the articulation and implementation of the school's ethos.

Chaplains' Association Groups

Finding a common means of support is critical not only for the chaplain at a personal level but it is also essential for the effective working of the ministry. The work of the School Chaplains' Association has been crucial in providing a range of support structures to chaplains throughout the country. On a smaller scale, as well, chaplains often meet one another in order to share concerns, ideas and resources. Much can be gleaned from the learning experience of others, especially in local group settings. One significant means of support is to gather together, as the following example of ten chaplains who met frequently demonstrates:

Small Group Meeting of Chaplains

Format: each meeting begins with a short prayer led by the convener. The meeting falls into three sections: 1) practical, 2) general, 3) personal. Time for a meal together, big or small, is an important social factor worth considering.

Practical: the first section begins with a presentation by one or two of the participants on some area of significance for chaplaincy work, e.g. reconciliation services, prayer, working with parents, retreats. This serves as a focus for discussion as well as offering useful ideas and a pool of resources.

General: the second section focuses on general issues such as confidentiality and referrals, adolescence and faith development, the religious education syllabus.

Personal: the third section is an opportunity for chaplains to share any aspect of the role, perhaps, by using one of the following headings as a guide:
- an enriching experience.
- a concern I have.
- advice I need.

Training of Chaplains

This handbook demonstrates the many facets of the role of chaplain showing that it is not a ministry to be entered into lightly. Despite the great work of chaplains in the field, the ministry has often been the victim of a hit and miss mentality. Like every other profession, proper training is essential, but until recently evidence of satisfactory training programmes is scant. Fortunately, however, in recent times much has been happening to change this situation. In Dublin, for example, pioneering work is taking place in the Mater Dei Institute of Education. Here, along with formal training, personnel who show a particular aptitude for the ministry are encouraged to embark on its pastoral/academic programme. Other diocesan and religious orders throughout the country also offer significant training and ongoing support opportunities.

Issues in training

The complex nature of the role of the chaplain demands careful preparation by those undertaking the work. Be aware, however, that this should not happen in an elitist way. Remember that any chaplain might be called upon to respond to the needs of those from secular as well as faith-based backgrounds. Despite the variation of needs, seldom has there been a more wonderful opportunity for evangelisation and catechesis in this country. The unique opportunity afforded should be seized by those responsible for the training and appointment of chaplains. Normally, those involved in the formation of chaplains tend to concern themselves with the following issues:

- *faith development.*
- *inter-personal skills.*
- *collaborative ministry.*
- *ecumenism.*
- *secularism.*
- *local church involvement.*
- *study of theology.*
- *personal development.*
- *youth ministry.*
- *supervised placement experience.*
- *basic counselling & spiritual direction.*
- *leadership and team work.*
- *liturgical celebration.*
- *sensitive and legal issues.*
- *school ethos.*
- *national education policy & provision.*

Personal

It is within the context of these support structures that awareness of one's own personal needs should be considered. Cooperation and collaboration with these structures will not be possible if the chaplain fails to address or reflect upon his/her own personal needs. As with all human beings, the chaplain is well advised to be conscious of what is happening at the different levels of his/her own life. This is a key practice to be developed particularly in relation to ministry. The following questions, therefore, might be worthy of your consideration:

Personal needs of the chaplain:
− am I overworked? .
− is too much expected of me?
− where can I talk about my troubles?
− how do I cope with working in teams?
− do I have time to deepen my own faith?
− do I take time to read and keep up to date?
− do I feel I have to be all things to all people?
− do the burdens of others consume my energy?
− is it my needs or the needs of the school that drive my ministry?

Take action

From being conscious of the issues and concerns above, it now becomes necessary to address them. What is required is the development of a habit of supporting the self rather than a habit of neglecting the self. Again a range of strategies suggest themselves:

Some Suggestions

Meeting personal needs

Having reflected upon your needs in terms of personal support, prioritise the following, decide *what* you are going to do and *when:*

- begin spiritual direction.
- join a chaplains' support group.
- plan a personal retreat.
- take some relevant in-services courses.
- seek assistance on the development of a role definition.
- structure some regular time off.
- set aside time for reading and research.
- link in with diocesan/congregational supports.

To reflect upon

What forms of relevant support are available to you?

What can you do to ensure you receive the support you require?

How can you encourage others to support you?

Special Concerns

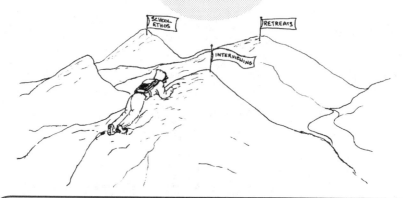

It is hoped that many pertinent issues have been addressed in this handbook so far. However, while the handbook is not all-embracing of the many and various concerns of school chaplaincy, some important matters still require attention. We will now focus on three which are most worthy of consideration. You will find these under the following headings: retreats, individual interviewing and ethos.

Retreats

Retreats offer a unique opportunity for spiritual and religious awareness and development. Well designed programmes and suitably trained personnel will make a considerable contribution not only to the ethos of the school, but also to the religious education already being provided by the religion team. Retreats are not intended to be just 'one day wonders'; they are an integral part of the spiritual life of the school community. It is essential to ensure that they are of such quality that they integrate with the life of the school environment. Preparation, participation and evaluation by and of personnel offering the retreats is vital. While retreats contribute to the whole development of the person, they emphasise the spiritual and religious dimensions in particular. For some practical suggestions in this respect, see 'school retreat guidelines' in chapter 9. These resources indicate the various ways chaplains might become involved in the retreat.

Reconciliation and Eucharist

The celebration of Reconciliation and Eucharist is perceived as a key experience in any retreat programme. The richness offered through carefully planned and sensitively celebrated liturgies cannot be overstated.

Reconciliation celebrates the mercy of God in our lives . Within this context, the students are invited to recognise their need of healing and to welcome the ever-present forgiveness and love of God. Chaplaincy, of its nature, is about taking various initiatives to celebrate the Sacrament of Reconciliation in as many ways as possible. Above all, it is especially desirable that senior cycle students be given the opportunity to celebrate reconciliation sacramentally.

Eucharist celebrates the love of God for us. Eucharist recognises the special *presence* of God in the gathering of the community, in the proclamation of the Word and in the bread and wine transformed. A more fitting means of bringing together the work of the retreat does not exist. Careful and participative preparation and involvement ensure the most fruitful experience. On occasion, however, it may be inappropriate to celebrate Eucharist if there is a danger that it might lead to disrespect for the sacrament. Nonetheless, this does not exclude some liturgical experience being offered as a means of proclaiming God's goodness.

Prayer

Retreats contribute to the work of religious education in helping the students not only to know *about* God, but also to develop a personal relationship *with* God. Like any relationship, a relationship with God must be expressed in dialogue and fostered through constant communication. Teaching young people to pray must be a part of every retreat. Students, therefore, need to be invited to:

– contemplate awareness of God's presence.
– learn to be comfortable with silence.
– reflect and listen to God and become aware that God is always listening to them.
– experience the many forms of the church's prayer.

The different prayer forms used on retreat should foster attitudes of praise, joy, awe, thanks, love, intercession and reverence. The witness of adult prayer is vital especially in the senior years.

The role of the school chaplain

Retreats offer a unique opportunity for the chaplain to be a spiritual presence to the student. The chaplain should participate in some way in the retreat programme. This involvement might include the following:

* careful planning with the religious education co-ordinator.
* meeting with the retreat team prior to retreat.
* availability to meet pupils during retreat.
* involvement with the celebration of sacraments.
* following up on issues raised during the retreat where appropriate.

Individual Interviewing

With respect to individual interviewing, the school community must have a proper procedure set in place. The chaplain must know this procedure, live by it and contribute to its implementation.

Policy and Procedure

It is crucial for a school community to establish policy and procedures for the private interviewing of individuals which might need to be carried out by any of the school personnel. This policy would need to state:

* why individual interviews are necessary - where they are linked with school ethos - how they are linked to the care of the student - how they are rooted in the school's ethos.
* the purpose of particular interviews with the guidance counsellor, class tutor, principal, chaplain.
* the procedures to be observed in the carrying out of interviews.
* the process of referral, internal and external.
* procedures for handling difficulties that may arise as a result of the interview process.
* a mechanism for reviews of the policy.

The chaplain – significant adult

Clearly, then, one of the ways in which the chaplain becomes a *faith presence* to young people is to be available for individual accompaniment. Students will often need dependable adults to talk to during the years at school. At one time the need might be of a spiritual nature and at another time the need will arise from problematic areas of life. Being able to trust a significant adult at times like these is of crucial importance to young people. In schools where a caring environment is functional, students can depend not only on the chaplain but also on a whole range of people. They might turn for assistance, for example, to a favourite teacher, the guidance counsellor, the year head, the class tutor. However, the chaplain, whose ministry lends itself to being of assistance in personal matters, should be the most accessible and willing of all staff members. The chaplain, therefore, will:

> * encourage students to be open with the appropriate adults.
> * encourage teachers to support students.
> * have a clear understanding of referral.

Interviewing and the chaplain

Each chaplain will have a unique approach when it comes to the business of interviewing. Some, because of their training and experience, will be in a position to offer this service on a wider scale than many of their colleagues. Others, who are not qualified to interview in specifically sensitive areas, should refer the case immediately to appropriately qualified personnel.

Regardless of the nature of the difficulties expressed by individuals, it is vital that the chaplain reflect carefully on the process to be taken. For example:

Clarify the reason for the individual interview
How does it fit with school policy?
How do I make this clear to students, staff and parents?

Discuss your role in this area with the pastoral team
What do they see as the needs?
What support do you require from them?
Could any of the less confidential interviews be done in pairs?

The principal and guidance counsellor need to have a significant input
Have you clear lines of communication with the guidance counsellor?
Are the referral procedures clear, working in practice and reviewed?
Has the principal approved your personal policy and procedures?
What form does your accountability take in this area?

Be clear on the policies concerning sensitive/difficult issues
What is the procedure in cases of sexual abuse, bullying, expulsion?

Spiritual focus and the whole person
The chaplain is concerned with the development of the person as a whole. When individual interviewing takes place, there must be a recognition of the importance of faith as it integrates with life. Again the Emmaus Story reminds us of the chaplain's role as one which offers individual accompaniment to everyone who requires it. Be aware that it is only when spiritual experience is understood in relation to lived experience that faith will truly speak to the individual.

Some Suggestions

Procedures: have a clear and consistent procedure for individual interviews.

Appointments: how appointments are made; appointment slip given and countersigned by releasing teacher and held for records.

Confidentiality: (outside the sacrament) the level of confidentiality needs to be clearly communicated to students. It is not appropriate to offer complete confidentiality. Clarify that in cases where either the student or some other person is in danger you will need to consult others about the situation. To the best of your ability you will negotiate the *how* of this consultation with the student. The assistance of the guidance counsellor is crucial.

Record-keeping: it is important to keep a brief record of each meeting. This may be of use later when seeing the student again or in the case of a query arising out of the meeting.

Referral: the school needs to have a clear policy in this area. Normally, it is not acceptable for the chaplain to assume the role of counsellor except where that has been agreed by the principal and the other school personnel with appropriate training. Referral can be either internal or external. In general this referral is operated through the guidance counsellor and occasionally through the principal.

School Ethos

School ethos is defined as follows for the purposes of this handbook:
  1) the ethos is the expression of the school's core values.
  2) it determines the character of the school community.
  3) it guides the daily life and direction of the school.

The trustees of a school have primary responsibility for the implementation of its ethos. For example, in a school under the trusteeship of a religious order its ethos will be rooted in the faith as expressed by the particular charism of that congregation. It is vital that the school's ethos does not remain an ethereal concept but finds expression at every level of school life.

Operational values

In every environment where people are interacting and working together, values, attitudes and behaviour determine its climate. In a school setting each member of that community brings a set of values, attitudes and behaviours into the school. Remember that there is no such thing as a 'value free' society or belief. The society in which the school is set also contributes significantly to the climate of the school. The ethos of a school is, in its turn, a vital and fundamental contributor of values, attitudes and behaviours. It is, therefore, crucial that schools continually examine these operational values to ensure that the ethos is neither submerged nor sidelined. Indeed, these values should be visible in the day-to-day interactions and decisions of the school.

A reflection on fundamentals

These are some sample questions that may be useful when reflecting on operational values and the place of school ethos:

* what values underpin the relationships in the school?
* what conclusions can we draw from the behaviour of our students regarding their attitudes to learning, justice, cooperation, competition, care?
* when examining our school policies on entrance procedures, behaviour code and curriculum choice, what values direct these policies?
* are there opportunities for all in the school community to reflect upon and contribute to the future direction of the school?
* are we happy with the values, attitudes and behaviour that characterise our school on a day-to-day basis?
* what other values might we consider that would better suit the needs of our school?
* how can a better articulation of our school ethos assist us in creating the type of school where each person is respected, valued and nurtured?

Role for the chaplain

While the chaplain has much to contribute to school ethos, it is important not to assume sole responsibility for it. The school's ethos is a matter for the entire school community. All have a role to play in ensuring fidelity to this ethos and its creative expression in the day-to-day life of the school. The chaplain, nonetheless, takes special care to be a resource person in this matter.

Some Suggestions

These suggestions may involve the chaplain to varying degrees. Each of the contexts below determines the extent of the chaplain's involvement.

Special Ethos Programme for Students: develop a series of classroom materials that can be used by teachers in order to discuss and familiarise students with the ethos. This programme could be cross-curricular, finding obvious connections with Social, Personal and Health Education (SPHE); Civic, Social and Political Education (CSPE); Religion, English, History, Geography.

School Ethos Day: perhaps use the school's saint or dedication day as a focus to hold a range of ethos related events: poster competitions, prayer services, talks to parents and staff, special school prayer to start each class.

Assemblies: the chaplain might prepare a special input; involve others in the school's ethos and its application to daily life in the school.

School Decoration: the environment of the school is a significant indicator of the atmosphere of the school. It may be worthwhile to use symbols, drawings and posters depicting the ethos to decorate the building.

Formation of School Policies: it is essential that the ethos centrally informs key policies such as entrance procedures, behaviour code and curriculum choice.

Staff Liturgy: the key implementors of the school's values are the staff. It is essential that the ethos is communicated to this group so that they can creatively interact with it as they work with the students. Perhaps, you could make the ethos the focus of an annual staff liturgy.

A Speaker: invite a person who has an insight into the area of ethos, or who has a special appreciation of the school's particular ethos – a past-pupil, teacher, religious, parent – to address staff and/or parents.

School Plan: many schools involve themselves in a whole school review and planning process. This entails the staff essentially but it also includes the parents and students as they examine every area of school life to create a better environment for learning. This process, often initiated by trustees, is founded on the school's making explicit its values and ensuring the consequent policies, structures and programmes. Ethos has a key role to play in the evolution of the school plan.

To reflect upon

1. What role might retreats play in your school?

2. What support do you need in respect of individual interviewing?

3. What steps can you take to promote the ethos of your school?

67

Death and Bereavement

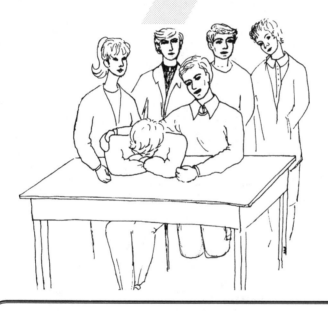

Dealing with death and bereavement is inevitable in any school environment but the manner in which it is approached will say a great deal about the school community. The chaplain, in particular, will find that it is probably more distressing than any other experience. Death and bereavement, above all, are the circumstances most likely to make demands on the chaplain as a *faith presence*. Given the uniqueness and individuality of each death and bereavement situation, it is possible only to make a few suggestions. Remember that judgement, sensitivity and intuition are vital on the part of the chaplain.

Visitation

Visiting the homes of the bereaved is a strong tradition in the Irish context. Depending on the response that each situation calls for, the chaplain will take a number of approaches. In the case, for example, of the death of a student's parent, the chaplain would consider the following:

- a personal visit.
- the chaplain accompanied by the teacher/class tutor and/or principal.
- bring a small number from the student's class.

A visit such as this expresses the sympathy of the school community. Offer whatever help is necessary with the funeral arrangements. If students are accompanying the chaplain, a phone-call in advance would be appropriate in case that situation might warrant a forewarning. Where students are to accompany the chaplain it would be best to discuss the visit with them beforehand as some might not have been previously exposed to major bereavement.

Accompaniment

Being available to those who are bereaved is a great service. Nonetheless the chaplain needs to be aware that there is no right or wrong time or way to grieve. For young people the experience can be particularly traumatic and much time and gentle encouragement is needed to help students find the appropriate expression for their grief. The chaplain's part is merely to provide opportunities to aid the healthy journey through grief. In this respect, being conscious of one's own response to personal grief is very important. As with many other areas of school life, be aware that support from and referral to other professionals is essential.

Whole school approach

Insofar as possible it is vital that structures and programmes are set in place to help the school community cope with major bereavements. The issue could be addressed in a variety of ways. In this context, a wide interpretation of the experience of bereavement and loss is useful. Both the *Rainbows* and *Spectrum* programmes, available to schools and parishes, are particularly helpful. Through these programmes, training is offered to parents and teachers who wish to work with young people as they experience death, loss and separation of a loved one. Some strategies which might be worthy of consideration are:

* a unit dealing with death and loss in the Social, Personal and Health Education course and Religious Education programmme.
* in-service for staff on issues around death and loss.
* special liturgy during November for past students and staff.

The death of a student

The death of a student is a most painful and traumatic experience for any school community. Although there is no blueprint on how to respond, the chaplain might be assisted by the case history outlined below. (Some details of the case have been altered.) As you reflect on the following course of action you might ask yourself these questions:

- what role would be most appropriate for me?
- what elements of this response am I uncomfortable with and why?
- what other approach could be taken?

John died in an accident late one evening. The school was informed the following morning. The principal, chaplain and class tutor discussed an initial plan of approach while other staff were informed and their support and advice was sought. It was agreed that the students would have to be told as soon as possible.

First of all, John's class needed to be given special attention. The class tutor went to John's class and asked them to accompany him to the oratory where the principal, chaplain and two other teachers joined the class. It was felt that the act of moving to the oratory would begin to prepare the class for the shock. The class tutor knew the students very well and he broke the news as gently as possible. The principal spoke and then the chaplain. The intention was to:

- communicate the news in a sensitive manner.
- give the facts as they were known.
- create a 'safe space' for the students to articulate the many ways they might react both immediately and in the long term.
- emphasise the support that would be available to them and how they might help each other.
- take time to pray for John, his family and friends.

The class was then asked what support they needed. They chose some time together in the oratory talking to each other while the teachers and chaplain stayed with them. Then they were given tea and coffee. They remained there for a while and those who felt the need to phone home were encouraged to do so.

While this was happening some teachers went around each class group before break time to inform the other students of the tragedy. During break time teachers went out to the schoolyard and mingled with students to offer support. As lessons resumed, teachers and students alike were talking and supporting each other.

It was decided that the chaplain and a teacher should visit John's home during the morning. This visit was difficult but the family very much appreciated the school community's thoughts and prayers. Their hearts were also somewhat lifted when they discovered that John's friends and the other students were being given support in their own respective grief at this sad time. This particular family welcomed any visit from the students over the following days. Before and after the visit, time was taken to talk with the students about the experience.

Back in school a decision was made to have an assembly before lunch break in order to unite the school community as it dealt with the shock of John's death. The bringing together of the student body was done without any difficulty. The chaplain and religious education co-ordinator prepared a simple prayer service consisting of a hymn, a reading and prayers of intercession. The principal introduced the service and the chaplain spoke for a few moments on:
- recognising the sense of loss.
- the many different ways we respond to loss.
- the importance of our prayers for those bereaved.
- our responsibility as a school community to watch out for each other in these sad days.
- the support that would be available to students.

The students from John's class and his other friends had free and readily available access to the chaplain, guidance counsellor and tutor for the remainder of that day and in the days following. The students, for their part, tended to come in small groups.

The removal and funeral were painful and desperately sad occasions while the class and John's friends were encouraged to gather and travel together. Before and after the ceremonies, both students and staff were involved in the guard of honour as well as other aspects of the funeral.

In the days following the funeral, John's class, as a group, requested to gather in the oratory to pray and talk about their experiences of grief and sadness. While this wish was respected the students were also encouraged to begin the process of integrating their school life with their sense of loss, confusion and pain.

A month later a one day retreat was organised for the class. Parental permission was sought and the retreat team were informed about the tragedy. The retreat proved a most healing experience for the class. The chaplain was present throughout the day and the class tutor joined the class for the special prayer time at the end of the day.

While the above case history offers only a brief outline of the tragedy and subsequent consequences, it may be helpful to you as you reflect upon the possibility of a tragic death in your school community.

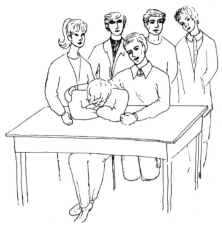

Care of bereaved students
A study by Ruth O'Rourke

The role of the chaplain in student experience of loss

The school chaplain, along with other members of staff, has a responsibility to promote the spiritual, moral, cultural, mental and physical development of students and prepare them for the responsibilities of adult life. A student may suffer many crises or experience many difficulties which may hinder this development. The chaplain must be aware of the flashpoints in the life of a student during which he/she may need support and help. One of these flashpoints may be a loss to the student through death, a heavy burden for the adolescent to bear.

Adolescent understanding of loss

Loss through bereavement can be especially traumatic because the adolescent is struggling with an emerging sense of self and all the uncertainties that are commensurate with this particularly vulnerable age. When bereaved, a conflict arises for the adolescent between wishing to appear self-sufficient and wishing to be comforted in his/her loss. This conflict can

73

give rise to apparent indifference or lack of feeling which can be puzzling to adults. The bereaved adolescent can experience anxiety, anger and depression which tends to manifest itself in deterioration of school performance, poor concentration/memory, and apparent sullen irritability.

Adolescents rely heavily on their peers for support. However, sometimes they refrain from sharing their grief with their friends because they feel that discussions about death may be potentially overwhelming. Bereavement is a social network crisis. The vacuum created by the loss of a significant relationship can throw an entire group into distress. Particularly, when the death of a peer occurs, the collective experience of suffering may render members of a group unable to support individuals for whom the loss is most immediate and profound. This is when the intervention of the chaplain can be of the greatest significance. Adolescents highly value the needs of their peers and feel very inadequate if they are unable to help each other.

Adolescent experience of death and loss
A survey was carried out, during the research for this paper, among transition year students and guidance counsellors in second level schools in 1997. The survey showed that 77% of transition year students experienced the loss of someone to whom they had been close. More than half of the students had been bereaved in the three years prior to being surveyed, while 16% had suffered loss through death before they were eight years old. 51% of the students surveyed approached someone to speak about their loss, while 62% of students were approached by someone offering to speak to them. This leaves a significant proportion of students who had suffered a bereavement neither having spoken of their loss nor having been given the chance to do so if they so wished. These are the students, in particular, to whom the chaplain could offer some time and a listening ear.

All of the students surveyed stated that their teachers and classmates were very supportive immediately after their loss. Both staff and students attended church services, sent Mass cards and floral tributes. However, when the bereaved students returned to school this level of support was not sustained. 90% of students indicated that they did not receive any help to settle back into their studies. This was despite the fact that 45% of

74

bereaved students said they were not coping well for a fortnight after they returned to school.

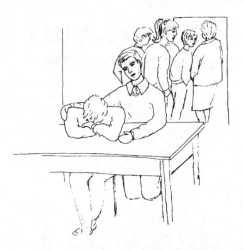

When the bereaved student returns to school

When the bereaved student returns to school the chaplain can help to smooth the path of the student back to the familiar rhythm of school-life. He/she may remind the teachers to be aware of the reason for the student's absence from class. The chaplain may enlist the help of classmates to keep the student up to date with work he/she may have missed. There is no set period of mourning in Irish society, so a student often returns to school within days of the loss. The chaplain can invite him/her to speak about the loss and other related difficulties that may be encountered in school. A service of remembrance, in a form chosen by the student, might be discussed and planned. It is of the utmost importance that the student is aware that someone is available when the need to talk arises. Helping bereaved people to express sorrow seems to aid recovery.

> Give sorrow words; the grief that does not speak
> whispers the oer-fraught heart and bids it break.
> *Macbeth (1v iii)*

Safe Harbours
Michael Martin OFM

Roused from myself
I take up my position
again facing the shore.

Taking the odd glance back across the horizon,
watchful,
I know it is there
that there will be campfires
and home from the sea stories

I know you will be there too.

But for now there is the horizon
and the other travellers on board.

I see your face come into view
and feel the shadow of your story
your life, unfinished
so full of possibility.
Listening is all we share
keeping our nerve in this moment's intimacy.

The call to be human
as Christ was
eating that bit of fish
that day we stopped off
just to get directions
to check that it was safe to go on.

The fear of God,
the love of God,
the unknown God,
the Trinity of you and me
and the ever present, distant shore.

Resource Ideas

Beginning a Conversation

The following is a possible format for initiating a conversation with students. The chaplain would visit a class, explain the role of chaplain and then ask the students to fill in the handout opposite. Remember to emphasise the confidentiality of it. Students should be advised that they need only complete the questions they wish. If they are comfortable they might discuss what they have written or anything else when they visit the chaplain.

Complete the sentences in your own words:

Name: **Class:**

1. What I think school is about ....
2. My class...
3. Where I live...
4. Things I like..
5. I am best when...
6. Getting on with people..
7. I wish others would..
8. The one thing I'd change...
9. I sometimes worry about...
10. I regret..
11. God is like..
12. About Jesus I don't understand...
13. Being a Christian means...
14. Confession...
15. Mass..
16. I'd like to ask God...
17. Prayer is..
18. My parents..
19. The rest of my family...
20. Something else I'd like to add...

Note

It is important that the choice of questions is agreed with the religion teacher and the guidance counsellor. Clarity on the referral procedure is required. This strategy is not for the purposes of counselling but as a possible means of spiritual accompaniment with students who wish to avail of this route as they deepen their faith.

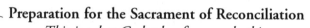

Preparation for the Sacrament of Reconciliation

This is what God asks of you, only this:
to act justly,
love tenderly
and to walk humbly with God. (Micah 6:8)

In our lives we experience, on the one hand, goodness, peace, joy and love, and on the other, evil, pain, suffering and hatred. Within each of us is the potential for good and for evil. It is difficult, even painful, to confront ourselves with the reality of our own lives and to take responsibility for the pain and suffering we have caused to others. God calls us to grow. We want to change, and we know we can. God wants us to know our gifts and to build on these. Through Jesus we are assured of God's love and forgiveness no matter how distant we might feel from God.

Being Honest Before God

Mark below the areas for which you feel the need to take responsibility and work on over the next while:

Forgiveness:

___Is there anyone I find difficult to forgive?

___Who or what makes me angry in my family life, my work life, my social life?

___Do I talk about and criticise people?

___Whom have I hurt by an angry word or action in my family or among my friends?

___Is there anyone in my family on whom I have given up?

Sense of wonder:

___Do I drink to excess?

___How does my drinking affect my family and my friends?

___Do I encourage others to drink more than they want?

___Do I take drugs?

___Do I encourage others to take drugs?

___Do I spend too much money on my own pleasure and entertainment?

___Do I gamble a lot?

___Do I grafitti property that is not mine? Do I vandalise property?

Appreciating myself:

___Do I try to recognise and improve the gifts and qualities I have?

___Do I neglect my health and not take exercise?

___Do I make it difficult for others to appreciate and care for me?

___Do I stand up for myself and my beliefs?

___Am I lazy?

___Am I giving myself enough time and energy to study?

Appreciating others:

___Do I slag and jeer others constantly?

___Am I jealous of other people?

___Can I be trusted in a relationship?

___Do I use other people?

___Do I respect the sexual dignity of myself and others?

___Do I try to look for and acknowledge what is positive in others?

___Do I treat others unfairly or steal what is not mine?

Inner life and God:

___Do I take time to figure out what values will guide my life?

___Do I thank God for my successes or just blame God for my failures?

___Do I respect others who 'walk with God'?

___Do I make an effort to understand and participate at Mass and
        Confession?

___Am I happy with the place God has in my life?

___Is there some other area I need to be honest about in the sight of
        God?

Hand this sheet to the priest you choose to speak with and talk about any of the items you have marked. If you wish, ask to see the priest for a longer chat at some other time.

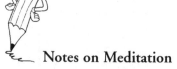

Notes on Meditation
Prayer and Meditation

A. Gospel Meditation

The work of Anthony de Mello and many others is invaluable in this area. One meditative approach is to quieten the self within a group context. In this way it is possible to achieve a reflective atmosphere for guided meditation on the gospel scenes. Meditation should include time for personal prayer as a means of engaging with the Lord. Participants might also be invited to share their experiences verbally and in writing.

B. Prayer and Meditation Group

Some chaplains find the response to prayer and meditation experiences so enthusiastic that they set up and facilitate prayer groups for senior students. One approach is to set up a group of about twenty students, encourage them to meet once a week for prayer, and ask them to commit themselves to regular prayer during the week. In the course of the weekly sessions, students are afforded the opportunity to discuss their experiences of the week. The use of a prayer journal is most helpful. Many resources are available for the setting up and running of such groups.

C. Forms of Prayer

School text books used in religious education generally have material containing the various forms of prayer as they are found in the Christian tradition. However, it is especially helpful when the chaplain suggests extra resources which might be of use to religion teachers. In this way the teacher will be practically prepared especially when it becomes necessary to respond to the many and various events in the life of the school community. Obviously you will find your own style; use the hints below to suit your particular situation. The following are just some pointers that have been found helpful by many:

1. Beginning: Start with small doses … in junior years put it to them as a challenge … will you be able to stay silent with eyes closed for one minute? … try again.

2. Music: Background music is invaluable for creating an atmosphere and blocking out the noise that may be around.

3. Take Time: Be patient … allow the giggles … Just encourage them to concentrate on the music … slowly they will quieten … if one or two are being difficult, quietly encourage their participation without disturbing the rest of the group.

4. Place: Go to to a different place if at all possible – the sanctuary of a church, a prayer room, a carpeted room. Always have an alternative exercise should meditation not work out.

5. Space: Try and spread students out; lying flat is good or with their backs against the wall. For your own sanity, separate obvious 'messers' – these, given the opportunity, are the ones who generally enjoy the prayer experience most.

6. Be aware: You will probably notice that one or two do not close their eyes. If after your normal encouragement they still don't, it is better not to force them as this could be an indicator of some difficulty. So long as they are not disturbing others, leave them be.

7. De-briefing: Some form of de-briefing is important. In certain circumstances it may be possible to chat to the group as a whole about the exercise. Some written expression is very helpful. At the back of their religion journals, make space for a section on meditation. They should be encouraged to write a description of the meditation. The following questions may be helpful:

> *What was good...what was difficult...what was strange...what was my dominant feeling...what did I learn...what image do I have of Jesus from this prayer time...is there a question I would like to ask?*

Look through these to give yourself a flavour of what's happening. It is good to remind the students that if anything comes up that 'upsets' them, they are free to approach you or another adult.

8. Small Groups: If at all possible take a half class size for meditation. This facilitates the development of an appropriate atmosphere.

Prayerforms for seniors

Aims:
1: To give students an experience of the different types of prayerforms which will enhance their personal spirituality.
2: To offer helpful suggestions for the graduation ceremony.

Prayerforms:
1. Taizé Prayer – use Taizé chants, scripture and intercessory prayer.
2. Meditation – guided gospel reflection with music.
3. Scripture Prayer – reflective reading of scripture with commentary. A large range of materials is available in this area.
4. Video – a short prayer video, for example, 'A Little Springtime', (Taizé video); 'A Way to God For Today', (Anthony de Mello).
5. Holy Souls Remembrance – each student is given a slip to write the names of those they want to remember, with a prayer service around this.
Procedure: Each group of 15 students will have 3 of the above experiences in a morning and/or afternoon. Allow 20 minutes for each session. The groups will move around the three different locations set up specifically for the prayerforms. Keep in mind the importance of creating an atmosphere suitable for reflection.
Follow-up: You may wish to offer an on-going prayer experience outside school time to students.

The Graduation Ceremony
The Graduation Ceremony is generally marked by a Eucharistic service as the sixth year students take their leave of post-primary education. Most students jealously guard the part they play in the planning of the liturgy. They often make it quite clear to teachers and chaplains alike that this is 'their Eucharist', 'their thanksgiving', 'their transition ceremony'. Therefore, they want a considerable say in the selecton of the theme, the readings, the Prayer of the Faithful, the music and the art work.

Sometimes, they even want to make a contribution at the homily time. Wise chaplains and teachers have learned to steer the students in a direction fitting for the Eucharist. The chaplain, then, should be present in a supportive and resourceful way as appropriate means are sought to recognise the transition that marks the end of their school lives and the beginning of the rest of their lives.

Some Suggestions

Student participation at every level is paramount for the liturgy.

* advance preparation by the students – a coordinating committee.
* penitential rite involving students, parents and staff.
* relate the choice of readings to the expressed needs of the students,
      e.g. celebration, thanksgiving, forgiveness, creativity, optimism.
* presentation of symbolic gifts.
* student commentator on the liturgy.
* invite parish clergy and personnel.
* a time-line picture gallery of events involving the graduating students.

Student Prayer Card

This prayer format can be well presented – perhaps in small card form – and given to senior primary or first year post-primary students at assembly or in class groups, with a short explanation by the chaplain. The prayer card might also be given to parents.

Daily Prayer Guide

Morning

In the name of the Father, and of the Son, and of the Holy Spirit.

Begin with this prayer of St Francis:
This day, Lord, where there is hatred let me bring forgiveness,
where there is sadness let me bring joy,
where there is need let me bring generosity.
Amen.

Now ask God, in your words, to bless the day ahead – that you might know God is with you *all through the day.*

Try and think of one good thing you would like to do during the day and ask for God's help in doing this.

Finish with the prayer:
Glory be to the Father and to the Son and to the Holy Spirit;
as it was in the beginning, is now and ever shall be,
world without end. Amen.

Daily Prayer Guide

At Night

In the name of the Father, and of the Son, and of the Holy Spirit.

Begin with this prayer:
Lord, it was you who created my inmost self,
and put me together in my mother's womb;
for all this I thank you;
for the wonder of myself and for the wonder of all your creation.
Amen.

Now think back on the day that's just over. What are you happy about? Is there anything you're sorry for? Talk to God in your own words.

Think of people you would like to pray for. Ask that God would bless each of them.

Finish with the Our Father.

Reflection on Psalm 139

This reflective prayer takes Psalm 139 for its inspiration. The prayer could be put on a card and read reflectively with a group before being given to those participating in the prayer.

Yahweh, you examine me and know me
you know if I am standing or sitting,
you read my thoughts from far away,
whether I walk or lie down,
you are watching, you know every detail of my conduct.

Lord, you tell me that you are near to me. Do I have the courage to recognise your presence, to recognise that it is a presence that is all merciful, all loving?

The word is not even on my tongue,
Yahweh, before you know all about it;
close behind and close in front you fence me round,
shielding me with your hand.
Such knowledge is beyond my understanding
a height to which my mind cannot attain.

That you, the Almighty God, show such intimate care for each of us, stretches my belief – help my unbelief.

Where could I go to escape your Spirit?
Where could I flee from your presence?
If I climb the heavens, you are there,
there too, if I lie in Sheol.

No matter where I stray in life, you promise to be there for me. May I never forget this truth and know always I can return to you.

It was you who created my inmost self,
and put me together in my mother's womb;
for all these mysteries I thank you:
for the wonder of myself, for the wonder of your works.

I take for granted the complex nature of my being, of my creation, of the great journey from conception. You, O Lord, have been with me all this time.

You know me through and through,
from having watched my bones take shape
when I was being formed in secret,
knitted together in the limbo of the womb.

This is a special time to bring to mind the wonder of my very self: the wonder of my being in the womb, the wonder of that self-same person — now many years on. You walk with me on the journey of life. I can choose to recognise your presence or, if I wish, to ignore it. This is an awesome gift of freedom. What will I do with this gift?

God, how hard it is to grasp your thoughts!
How impossible to count them!
I could no more count them than I could the sand,
and suppose I could, you would still be with me.

Lord you are Almighty, all-powerful, all-loving — yet you seem so hidden at times in my life. Do I know why this is? Yet you are there when I am ready to be with you. How will knowing about you and your love change my life? Am I afraid of what living your love really means?

God, examine me and know my heart,
probe me and know my thoughts;
make sure I do not follow pernicious ways,
and guide me in the way that is everlasting.

Lord, may the path of life I follow provide the opportunities for me to experience love to its greatest depths and may I offer to others the love of commitment, care and justice.

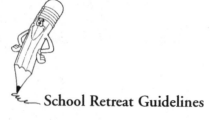

School Retreat Guidelines

Introduction

Many members of school communities are growing in their awareness of the value of a good retreat experience. With varying degrees of success, this awareness has led to different styles of retreats being availed of. Help from the chaplain is essential in this area. When the request from people who are concerned with retreats in your school is made, you may find the following guidelines or signposts particularly useful. Perhaps you might reflect on these in the context of your own situation.

Guiding principles

a. A retreat must have the spiritual as its focus. It recognises and acknowledges the human context of the students but goes beyond this to the faith context.

b. Retreats in the junior years have been found to be some of the most effective in the work of faith experience and learning. This seems to be due, in part, to a greater openness from the students.

c. Because chaplains and catechists are often in the business of difficult and isolating work, they are greatly encouraged by the support of good retreat personnel. In addition, it is desirable that students be offered the experience of people other than the familiar chaplain and catechist while they are on retreat.

e. In order to clarify expectations of retreat programmes, dialogue is essential between retreat personnel, catechists, chaplains, principals and students.

f. Parents need to become more and more involved in the process. This can be achieved through: information evenings run by the school and/or retreat personnel, newsletters to parents, interested parents involved in drawing up retreat programmes, retreats for parents.

g. Financial concerns – a workable system needs to be clarified from the outset. This could be 50% from students, 50% from the school. Other sources might be forthcoming, such as fund-raising by parents, students, a donation from involved parishes.

Retreat Programmes year by year

The following are suggestions to guide retreat personnel in their planning of a retreat experience. Discussion of these by all concerned is encouraged in order to maximise the retreat potential.

First Year:
Theme: Creating Christian Community: This will recognise the newness of second level school, bonding as a class and so forth. The sacraments of initiation will also be a key focus. The needs of this year group may be filled by a half day's experience with preparation work having been done in the religion class. The half day could be spent celebrating Eucharist with the school chaplain and a short pilgrimage to a local site of spiritual significance.

Second Year:
Theme: Our central place in God's creation: This theme, as in other years, is linked to the religious education syllabus. It includes issues such as the wonder of God's creation, our responsibility towards it, our special place in God's plan, our personal giftedness, our relationship with God. Crucial to the retreat experience will be developing the prayer life of the students by providing guided opportunities of experiential prayer. A celebration of Reconciliation and Eucharist will be a key part of the day, using the central theme to guide the style and content.

Third Year:
Theme: being responsible in my relationships: What do the values of the gospel teach? Examining the relationships of the student with God, family, peers and the earth. Provide opportunities for the Christian story to speak to these relationships. Prayer, Reconciliation and Eucharist are essential to this retreat day as a way to celebrate and challenge the students' approach to relationships.

Fourth Year:

Theme: Finding my place in the world: This transition year is one of exploration of one's gifts and talents. The retreat needs to echo the experiential nature of this year, perhaps by offering a retreat away from normal surroundings, such as a retreat house, working with the disabled, insight into the lives of the homeless. The retreat helps students to see God in so many ways and in particular how they can be the instruments of God's work on earth.

Fifth Year:

Theme: Exploring my journey with God: Enabling students to reflect on their experience of faith, helps and hindrances they experience, the doubts and questions they have. In fifth and sixth year the personal faith witness of the retreat team will be of crucial value.

Sixth Year:

Theme: Values for living: In this final year the students reflect on how they hope to live their lives. What will give meaning, direction and purpose? Interwoven into this reflection is the invitation of the Christian story to choose the values of Christ. The liturgy of Reconciliation and Eucharist are central to the experience.

Evaluation

It is important to take time with all those involved to review the experience of the retreat. This will need to be done with the retreat personnel, the students and the teachers concerned.

Finally, good retreat teams are booked early – so do your homework!

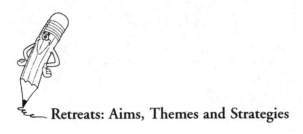

Retreats: Aims, Themes and Strategies

As a further support to chaplains we now outline some detailed aims and strategies for school retreats:

First Year

Aims:
1. To help first year students to adjust to a new school environment.
2. To recall their Confirmation experience and build on it.
3. To build up their self esteem.
4. To create a good class spirit.
5. To bring together the themes of the day in the celebration of the Eucharist.

Themes:
Newness, change, friendship, friendship of God, exploration of journey since Confirmation, association with the Child Jesus in the Temple, Eucharist as celebration – reconciliation, effective listening.

Strategies:
- Comparisons between being senior at primary and junior at secondary.
- Encourage quiet reflection on self.
- Story of the Child Jesus in the Temple.
- Remember and tell your Confirmation story.
- Discuss in small group, large group – nicknames, slagging, bullying, listening, and respect.
- Role-plays by retreat team on caring and listening skills.
- Preparation of the different parts of the Eucharist and celebration of the Sacrament of Reconciliation.

Second Year

Aims:

1. To encourage a sense of our own giftedness and respect for each other.
2. To build up self esteem.
3. To create a good class spirit.
4. To bring together the themes of the day in the celebration of Eucharist.

Themes:

Liturgy and class bonding, slagging, bullying, issues involved in growing up, being special in God's eyes, giftedness, personal and spiritual self worth, worth of others, diversity of gifts in class group, Eucharist as celebrating our relationship with God and each other, reconciliation, meditation.

Strategies:

- Brainstorming on giftedness.
- Small group work where each person claims his/her own giftedness with the assistance of the leader.
- Small group work on improving class relationships.
- Meditation – prayer experience.
- Retreat Team input on God in their lives.
- Affirmations in small groups
- Each is encouraged to name the gifts of the others in his/her group.
- Preparation of the Eucharist and time of Reconciliation.

Third Year

Aims:

1. To explore pressures and influences involved in growing up.
2. To build up self esteem.
3. To create a good class spirit.
4. To bring together the themes of the day in the celebration of Eucharist.

Themes:

Who am I in relation to family, peer group and God? Class relationships, effective listening and other relationship skills. A prayer relationship with God. Eucharist and Reconciliation.

Strategies:

- Focus on issues of the day in Morning Prayer led by retreat team.

- Needs assessment – what are the concerns of the class, reflected back to the class at the discretion of the team.
- Large group work on peer pressure.
- Worksheet on 'God in my life' – witness from team.
- Exploring images of God, expression of same on paper, sharing in large and small groups about images of God.
- Affirmation in small groups.
- Meditation experience – prayer to connect themes to a personal relationship with God.
- Celebration of Eucharist and Reconciliation.

Fourth Year

Aims:
1. To encourage students to see their giftedness as a means of reaching out to those in need.
2. To explore the many ways the church supports those on the margins of society.
Themes and strategies:
It is recommended that transition year students are given a very different experience from that of other years. An opportunity should be offered to students so that they might explore their own ability to be of service to others in a Christian and church context.

Fifth Year

Aims:
(A two day retreat is suggested for the senior years.)
1. To enable students to explore their personal struggles at a deeper level.
2. To facilitate an understanding of the opposite sex.
3. To encourage responsible attitudes to their own sexuality and that of others.
4. To develop prayer through meditation.
5. To provide an opportunity for the Sacrament of Reconciliation by focusing on areas of their lives where growth and change are required.
6. To develop a personal understanding and involvement in the Eucharist.

Themes:

Students' possible struggles with peer group, experience of God, communication with God, dealing with conflict, boy/girl relationships, sexuality, Eucharistic celebration and personal reconciliation.

Strategies:

- Needs assessment, anonymous freedom to express personal struggles, reflected back to class at the discretion of the team.
- God, witness from team, God in my life as a young person, my values, my spiritual journey.
- Meditation, journeys with Jesus through the gospel stories.
- Invite class to express their prayer experiences, images of God, images of self in relation to the world and God.
- Discuss their understanding of God's presence or absence in their lives.
- Relationships, role-play, input from team on positive relationships.
- Discuss emerging sexuality, church teachings, responsibility, disappointments in relationships.
- Lengthy preparation of various parts of the Eucharist.
- Preparation and celebration of the Sacrament of Reconciliation.

Sixth Year

Aims:

1. To explore their experience of God in relation to themselves and others, locating where God is at present and will be in the future.
2. To focus students on the challenge of facing the future away from the security of school and home.
3. To focus on areas of their lives where growth and change are needed, by providing the opportunity for the Sacrament of Reconciliation.
4. Develop personal understanding and involvement in the Eucharist.

Themes:

Future, decisions, insecurities, change, moral choices, personal and social responsibilities, images of God, relationship with God, personal issues, male/female relationships, gender, listening to self, others, God.

Strategies:

- Explore the effects of popular culture on their lives with direction from the team.

- The future, input from the team, evaluation, decision-making, hopes and
    fears regarding future, discussed in small sroups.
- Quiet reflection, artistic expression of their past and future journey.
- Personal issues dealt with at the discretion of the team.
- Justice and peace, soap box discussion.
- God, prayer, meditation, witness from leaders, discussion in small groups,
    sharing experiences of God's presence or absence in their lives.
- Relationships, as for fifth year.
- Particular attention to affirmation as this is their last year together.
- Eucharist and Reconciliation celebrated as a culmination of a journey –
    related to the work of the two days.

Note on celebrating Eucharist and Reconciliation
The emphasis is put on celebration while the team uses its own creativity
to encourage the young people to make the sacraments an expression of
their own lives. The team strives to give them an experience of intimate
union with God.

Reconciliation

As far as possible, an opportunity for reconciliation should be provided. At
junior level the reconciliation service should be a simple event. Here members
might name some part of their lives where they need forgiveness and
where they receive absolution individually from the priest. At senior level,
it is suggested that the afternoon of the first day is given over to the sacrament
on a one-to-one basis. Use of ritual and symbolism here encourages
students and enriches the experience. Generally there is a very good
response to such special occasions.

Eucharist

The team should invite the class to decide on a theme for the celebration
of the Eucharist, especially where it might have related to their own experiences
of the retreat. All related, creative work should be included in the
Preparation of the Gifts and the class should pray for their own intentions
at the Bidding Prayers. It would be invaluable to have the school chaplain
closely involved both in the celebration and in the preparation of the service.

November Remembering

A Service for Sixth Class/First Year

Death and loss are issues that need to be addressed with every age group and to be integrated with our faith life. November has been the traditional month to bring to mind those who have gone before us. This service, which takes a class period, is best carried out in groups of 12-15 and, if at all possible, in the school oratory.

Prayer space: Prepare the space for the service – chairs in a circle, a prayer focus, a large lighted candle, smaller candles for the students, cards for students to write names, music playing as the students gather. (Suggestion: *O Lord Hear my Prayer,* Taizé.)

Introduction: A few short words setting the context of the service – remembering those whom we have known who have gone before us: family and friends. Remember also those who have no one to pray for them. Now ask students to write the names of people they would like remembered on the cards provided.

Reading: Luke 7:11-17. *The Widow of Naim.*

Candle lighting: Each student in turn is invited to call out one or more names from their card and to light their small candle from the central candle and place their candle on their card in the centre of the floor. When everyone is finished, a period of silence follows, perhaps with music played in the background. (Either *O Lord Hear my Prayer* from Taizé or the hymn *Shepherd me O Lord.*)

Reflection: You may wish to ask each to reflect on the good qualities of those whom they are remembering … which of these would they like to develop more in their own lives? … considering how they will make the most of the life that they now have. End this section with the Our Father said together.

Final Prayer: Loving God, we thank you for the opportunity to come together with you to remember those of our families and friends who have gone before us. We trust in your love for all people and pray that each of those we have remembered will always be in your loving presence and that we may know and share your love at all times during our lives. This prayer we make through Christ Our Lord.

A Sample Brochure

The following is the text of a brochure synopsising the work of the chaplain and the chaplaincy team in Killinarden Community School, Dublin. It may serve as a sample for those wishing to inform students, staff and parents of the place of chaplaincy in the school community.

Format: The brochure may consist of useful information which may be printed on to an A4 sheet of paper or fine cardboard and folded breadthways into three parts.

Page 1: (front cover):
- Name of School.
- A suitable logo.
- Chaplaincy team.
- A short scripture quotation.

Page 2: The Chaplaincy team
The Chaplaincy Team at KCS is composed of the School Chaplain and professionally trained volunteers from the Sacred Heart Parish, Killinarden, who work together with professional Youth Workers from the Catholic Youth Council, the YMCA and the Tallaght Youth Service.

The Chaplaincy Team at KCS can be described under four headings:
- Ministry to the students.
- Ministry to the family of the students.
- Ministry to the staff.
- Ministry through the liturgy.

Open door
No matter what stage in life we are at, all of us need some kind of support. The Chaplaincy Team at KCS provides an open door where students can come and receive support in a confidential and safe way.

Many students have used this open door as their first step to dealing with a problem or seeking help. At times the Chaplain may think another member of staff or counsellor may be of help to the student and, with permission, may refer them to another support person. The School Chaplain works closely with the Guidance Counsellor and the Home-School Links Co-ordinator, as well as Class Tutors and Year Heads.

Page 3: Bereavement Support

The loss of someone close through death or separation is one of the most traumatic events in a person's life. When the loss occurs during teenage years the effect can be even greater.

The Chaplaincy Team at KCS provides a full bereavement support service through individual counselling and support groups. The bereavement support groups are facilitated by the School Chaplain and a qualified Bereavement Counsellor.

Let's Celebrate

Prayer and thanksgiving are an important part of a Christian's life. The Chaplaincy Team provides each student with opportunities to learn about new ways of talking to God. In the School Prayer Room class groups are offered prayer experiences which help to develop their relationship with God. Classes take part in Eucharistic Celebrations, Prayer Services and Meditation, thus making prayer a part of the ordinary life of the school.

G.I.F.T.

The *Growing in Faith Together* programme involves local parishioners sharing their own experiences of Christianity with students over six weeks. In turn the young people begin to learn how to talk about what their faith means to them.

Page 4: Retreats – Time Out

The Chaplaincy Team at KCS provides a full retreat programme for students in 1st, 3rd and 6th year. The retreats provide the students with an opportunity to reflect on their lives in relation to the issues they face each day and where God fits into their daily lives.

The retreat teams combine professionally trained volunteers with experienced professional retreat directors who have worked with young people in schools all over Ireland.

Youth Development
Behind the many activities of the Chaplaincy Team at KCS is the basic belief that each student has emotional, educational, physical and spiritual needs. The pastoral care offered by the chaplaincy Team at KCS seeks to develop the students at each of these levels.

In cooperation with the YMCA, the Chaplaincy Team provides young people with the opportunity to gain the skills and knowledge to develop themselves and their fellow students around issues such as north-south reconciliation and drugs education.

The Chaplaincy Team and the Tallaght Youth Service organise a weekly youth group which works to develop the students self confidence and life experience.

Page 5: Faith Friends
Each year approx. 120 young people are confirmed as young Christian adults in the Parish of Killinarden. As part of their preparation for this important event in their lives, 5th year students from KCS are trained by Religion Teachers to share their own faith with the candidates for Confirmation.

Gospel for Life
Each Tuesday afternoon a group of parents come together to meet in the School Prayer Room to reflect on their lives in the light of the gospel. With the School Chaplain they grow in their understanding of what it means to live the gospel message in the routine of our daily lives.

After hours ...
The School Chaplain is available to visit students and their families at home, as well as being a member of the Killinarden Youth Forum and the Killinarden Youth Club Committee, both of which meet in the Killinarden Community Centre.

Important!
In order that all of the students receive the greatest amount of care and support, it is very important that members of staff inform the School Chaplain immediately if a student is sick at home/hospital or if they are bereaved in any way.

Page 6:
 - The name of the school chaplain.
 - The names of the chaplaincy team.

The School Chaplain works closely with all members
of the School Staff as part of the overall
Pastoral Care offered at KCS.

KCS Prayer

God our Father, your Son Jesus lived in this world to show us that all life is important to you. Help us to use our gifts in ways that will help us and those around us to live life to its fullest.

Be with us when we are hurt and alone, and let your Holy Spirit give us the wisdom to know right from wrong, and the courage to love God and to love our neighhour as we would like to be loved ourselves. Amen.

St Vincent de Paul, Patron of our School, pray for us.

(Reprinted by kind permission of Fr James Norman, chaplain to Killinarden Community School, Dublin)

Reflections

Ten Years on
Luke Monahan

The following are some stray thoughts concerning my experience of being a school chaplain over ten years. I have been in two schools in that time, one co-educational and the other all boys. These few pages are an attempt to chart the learning for my role as chaplain. I can honestly state that the learning predominately arises out of the many mistakes I have made – so there is hope for those fortunate enough to be invited to take on this ministry!

Throughout this handbook, the Emmaus Story has been a focus for approaching chaplaincy. The Lord meets us in our present reality and from there invites us to journey with him. The chaplain needs continually to reflect on the ministry so that it becomes an ongoing response to the call of the Lord rather than an unconscious process of stagnation. As you ponder on this personal reflection, you might use the following questions and points as tentative suggestions for your own situation.

With regard to each point outlined below consider:
- is this area a concern in my context?
- what can I learn that may be of relevance to my faith and/or my ministry?
- what am I doing right in this sphere at present?

Lose the messiah complex...

You cannot change the world but you can change yourself. Chaplains do little service to a school by setting up initiatives which subsequently collapse on their departure. The belief that everything has to be done at once and by the same person, the chaplain, is all too familiar. A keen awareness that only so much can be done by any one person is a guiding principle which is worthy of consideration. A chaplain must have a set of values such as: enablement, empowerment, delegation and openness to learning.

Witness

The way you interact with all the members of the school community is the way you most significantly demonstrate your values. This is the key to the witness you give. You stand for the Good News, so demonstrate it, live it.

Spending Time

As a chaplain I have always believed the most valuable contribution I make to the school is simply that of *presence*. Being around the corridors greeting people, being prepared to waste time with people, is vital. Contrary to my 'busy' nature I have always found that spending time like this has been crucial to the development of my role in the school.

Not a Jack of all Trades

The chaplain should not feel the need to become an expert at everything, given that there are so many possibilities from which to choose in exercising the ministry. I soon found out that although I was not always the expert this was okay. I could let myself off the hook from 'being all things to all people'. As chaplain, play to your strengths and facilitate/support the provision of those services which you feel are outside your range of talents. For example, I was not good at school retreats, so I supported the setting up of a team of local people and helped to train them for this work. They became the school retreat team for our region. All I had to do was welcome them to the retreat, be around and say thanks! Needless to say, this does not excuse us from stretching ourselves and making an effort to improve the areas where we know development is possible.

Magpie

You do not have to re-invent the wheel when researching resources. Instead, you can be a collector of material or ask for resources from others. Watch out for ideas that work. All you have to do is figure out how they can be adapted to your situation. Keep a record of what you do from year to year so that you have a foundation on which to build. Also remember *you* are a resource person for others, so keep this in mind when you come across data which may not be of any specific use to yourself but it may be useful to others. You may be in a better situation than other staff members to compile material, so be aware of this advantageous position.

'I did it my way'

Chaplaincy and blueprints do not sit well together. Each of us has to find our own path in the chaplaincy ministry, which we can do by paying close attention to guidelines and pointers. Discover your own route and do not make apologies. This may seem very obvious but I have encountered so many chaplains who are completely driven by a force outside of themselves. They are constantly trying to fulfil the expectations of others by being all things to all people. All that happens is that they get burnt out in the process so – be yourself.

Be Aware

Be aware of the world of the students: what are their interests, do you know the difference between rap, rave and pop? What teams are big just now,

what expressions do they use? At the same time you cannot invent an interest that you do not have. Therefore, you need to build on those that you have. On a more serious level, some consideration is needed around the following issues:
- what is going on in adolescence?
- understanding the peer group.
- the effects of separation/bereavement/long term unemployment.

Become a student of their world, attend in-service training. Remember you will be a resource for other members of the school community as they strive to work with young people. Keep up to date on reading regarding education, chaplaincy, faith development. Constantly review your stance on these issues.

Prophet

In ministry we are called to be prophets of our times. This can be an uncomfortable role to exercise. Nonetheless, the chaplain sometimes has to be seen to stand apart, to declare the truth, to proclaim justice. In concrete terms, it may mean challenging teachers about an injustice regarding a student, or raising questions about the living out of the school's ethos. While having a responsibility to speak out, we also need to take care to present our message in a form that respects others and encourages a climate of dialogue.

Personal Integration

I finish with the dictum, 'be rooted in Christ'. He is your strength, your companion, your guide. Allow him to be that to you. Give time to this relationship, listen to how the Lord speaks to you in the events and relationships of your day, how you are being supported, how you are learning, how you are being challenged. Underpin this with the following supports:
- a spiritual director.
- a 'supervision' group to process the learning and to be supported both in your role as chaplain and at a personal level.

Reflections of a Principal
Elizabeth Cotter

The school chaplain is one of the key figures in the school community. Like the principal, the chaplain is called to respond to the unexpected, the unpredictable, the unplanned and the unstructured. Paradoxically, however, it is the chaplain's very ability to plan, structure and organise which determines his/her success in dealing with the crises which are the very stuff of everyday school life. For it is the planning, organisation and structure which gives the chaplain entré into every area of school life, thus preparing the ground for dealing with the unexpected.

The chaplain has all the benefits of the teacher with less of the drawbacks. The chaplain is not called to respond to the demands of the syllabus or to discipline students for their transgressions either academically or otherwise. Yet, his/her understanding of what goes on in the classroom gives the chaplain vital insight into the life of both student and teacher. This understanding also enables the chaplain to bridge the gap between the staff and the student membership and to be the facilitator of a good rapport between the two bodies.

Chaplaincy 'evolved' in my school during a period of nine years. Because the chaplain was an open person who was willing to take risks, the role in our school began to take shape over the years, culminating in a definite role description. As a result, I offer the following model as one which suits our school, but which may also prove useful to others who are in the process of working out the needs of their own schools.

In our school, the chaplain's areas of responsibility include the following:
1. Personal and spiritual development.
2. Liturgy and sacraments.
3. Pastoral and spiritual counselling.
4. Social justice outreach.

1. Personal and Spiritual Development

The chaplain accompanies students, staff and parents on their spiritual and human journey. This can be done by being available to help or provide assistance for those needing individual, personal or spiritual guidance. Availability, however, should be both formal and informal. Where it is formal there must be a structured schedule of work drawn up in consultation with the Principal. Where it is informal the chaplain should 'be around' areas where students congregate at breaks and lunch periods. The chaplain should also organise evenings of prayer/retreats for parents and staff, personal development programmes for students and parent programmes.

2. Liturgy and Sacraments

The chaplain is responsible for co-ordinating school liturgies, arranging class Masses, seasonal liturgies, Eucharistic or other services and Morning Prayer. He/she is also responsible for organising and preparing monthly Folk Group Liturgies for students and for the wider school community.

Further responsibility is in the provision of a variety of prayer experiences for students in collaboration with the R.E. team, the preparation of 6th year students for commissioning as Ministers of the Eucharist for service within both school and parish, ensuring the supply of altar breads, wine, candles and flowers. He/she is also responsible for highlighting liturgical seasons by offering services, talks, awareness exercises, visits and visual aids...

3. Pastoral and Spiritual Counselling.

The chaplain is responsible for implementing a systematic programme of contact with individual students. He/she must liaise with parents where appropriate and with the principal, guidance counsellor and pastoral co-ordinator. This is facilitated by weekly meetings. In addition, he/she will visit students, parents, staff who are in hospital, attend funerals, follow up visits with bereaved families and organise/provide bereavement counselling for students. He/she has special responsibility, in association with the pastoral co-ordinator and for the induction programme of new students.

He/she will liaise with parents and provide help/referral where required. He/she will organise a re-union for past pupils in association with the guidance counsellor during their first year out of school.

4. Social Justice Outreach

The chaplain promotes a spirit of concern for others within and beyond the school community. He/she promotes an understanding of and appreciation for Irish involvement in Third World projects. He/she co-ordinates pupil involvement in flag days and other fund-raising events for charities. He/she organises weekly meetings for the St Vincent de Paul Society, co-ordinates student parties for senior citizens at mid-term, Christmas and Easter, organises an annual Vincent de Paul sale of work, and helps students plan/organise Vincent de Paul week. He/she co-ordinates Transition Year student involvement in the Community Service Programme, pupil visits to the elderly, and co-ordinates student involvement in Social Justice Week and Mission Week. He/she supports the work of Amnesty International in which senior students are involved. The chaplain liaises with the parishes from which students come; he/she organises parish projects for first year students in association with the R.E. team early in the term.

The chaplain must be a 'people' person above all, one who is equally comfortable with adults and adolescents, since the role often calls him/her to mediate between the two. Personality would also be a key factor in the selection of a school chaplain. The chaplain's vision should be person-centred and holistic. He/she must be committed and enthusiastic, like being with young people, be comfortable liaising with their parents and teachers, and be warm, humorous and friendly. The chaplain needs to be able to work on his/her own, be able to manage time, be able to work as a member of a team, and be flexible and accountable. The chaplain should be a good listener, willing to be involved in the interests and activities of students both inside and outside school. At the same time, the chaplain must be willing to avail of opportunities presented for personal and professional development and growth. The chaplain must have the ability to be self-critical and be willing to participate in end of year evaluation when priorities are established for the coming year.

The successful chaplain takes care of him/herself professionally and personally. He/she is prepared to work with the Principal and other staff, especially pastoral personnel. He/she is willing to be part of the catechetical team within the school and to nourish and sustain the role by belonging to the Chaplains' Association outside of school. He/she is willing to undertake self-evaluation and also to be valued by Principal and school management. He/she is always seeking to ensure that the role is relevant to all the people currently involved in the school community. This means, above all, that the chaplain has no fixed ideas but is willing to seek and find possible solutions or ways of coping with sometimes insoluble difficulties.

If chaplaincy is to succeed in a school, management must be prepared to provide the resources necessary. Support structures must be put in place. If they are, the chaplain will be in a position to provide a vital service which is becoming more and more necessary in today's world. It has been my privilege to work with people who believe in the value of the chaplain's role. This belief has contributed in no small measure to the success of chaplaincy in Loreto College, St Stephen's Green.

Reflections of a Lay Person in Chaplaincy

David Kavanagh

The Rookie

My first day as a newly-appointed lay person working in the area of chaplaincy began last September. I spent the morning wandering around like a nomad, going from one group of teachers to another, feeling somewhat conspicuous. I tried to blend into the surroundings by acting confidently and speaking casually to people. As they began to accept me, my nerves began to dissipate. Queries such as, 'what will you do all day?', and, 'are you trained in chaplaincy work?', were among the most common of questions to be asked. Now, two months into the term, no one is surprised that chaplaincy ministry is not always carried out by an ordained man.

After that, the first few days were spent getting to know the students. On the one hand, I was not prepared to be seen as a loop through which they could jump in their daily struggle to avoid all things academic. On the other hand, however, my role in school is pastoral not academic. I have already found that one of the best ways to befriend the students is to become involved, where possible, in extra-curricular activities. Therefore, I set about organising a basketball league, sessions on learning the guitar, becoming a D.J. in our radio station, organising classes to sponsor children in Tanzania, teaching personal development classes, and setting up classes to counteract the possibility of bullying among the students.

The students

Also I piloted a new programme in the school whereby each sixth year has been assigned the task of looking after three or four first years. They meet once a week to ensure that the new students have adjusted to life in the school. Any difficulties encountered are dealt with by my fledgling student chaplaincy team. We meet once a fortnight to plan and review initiatives for the school. It is vital for students to be given an active and responsible role of this nature. The next stage is to develop and expand that role, thereby increasing student participation in pastoral care.

One of the greatest difficulties with which I have been faced has been my attempt to come to terms with the depth of suffering experienced by so many of the students. Death, loss and separation have affected over 60% of the young people in my school. This reality has reminded me that being a companion to both staff and students is a fundamental aspect of any pastoral work I undertake.

The parents

Another aspect of my role involves meeting the parents of the students. Recently I met with the parents of the first years to make them aware of my availability should they so wish. At this tender stage of my experience, I have already found out that the parents often need more support than the children. The promotion of harmonious relationships, where there is none, is just one of my long-term ambitions. Relationship is everything. It is the key to effective ministry.

A chaplain is someone to whom people can turn for warmth, kindness and affection but most of all for spiritual guidance. While this is not always going to be easy, I hope to learn more from experience as I continue in my new profession. To date I can say honestly that I am learning something new as each day dawns. Clearly, the potential and scope for involvement with young people is very wide but ultimately it depends on the right kind of encouragement and direction.

Reflections of a Voluntary Secondary Chaplain
John Kelly

When I first became voluntary chaplain to Ardscoil Rís secondary school six years ago, all I had was a boundless hope and a few skills. Therefore, the exceptionally warm welcome I received from the principal, R.E. team and staff is something for which I will always be grateful. Their welcome has made me feel part of the team and it has contributed enormously to my involvement in the life of the school. As a full time curate in a parish, my role as chaplain in the school was in a voluntary capacity. Little more was expected of me than that of sacramental ministry. However, I felt that I could not celebrate the sacraments unless I was part of the school community, sharing their joys and sorrows. Then, as now, I see my role very simply as 'being there' for the staff, students and parents. This includes responding to their needs, specifically by trying to mediate the compassion and love that Christ has for all people.

My focus as chaplain to the school community is person-centred. To the teachers and other staff members I see myself as a friend who offers support, compassion and encouragement as they struggle to meet the needs of the students. Together with their families, I have celebrated joyful and sorrowful times such as births, baptisms, marriages, sickness and death. To the students I see myself responding to what Merton Stronmen calls 'the five cries of youth', which are cries for love, support, belonging, guidance and friendship. Once I am satisfied that these five basic needs are being given attention I try to nurture the student's life of faith.

A day in the life of...

Given my parish duties, I can only spend one full day a week in the school apart from the times I come and go for specific sacramental reasons. Perhaps an overview of a typical day in the school might help those voluntary chaplains who are as unsure of themselves as I was six years ago. I might begin school with any given class group, offering a service of prayer. Breathing exercises and meditation would be part of the procedure. After a time of quietness, a reading would be shared followed by prayers and intercessions. The service would finish with an anointing of hands and a blessing for their work in the year ahead. This kind of service is always a bit of a gamble for any chaplain. However, the religion teacher might prepare the students in advance by encouraging them to take part respectfully in the service.

Once this class is over I would be likely to move to another class group. For example, I might go into a sixth year class. Part of the religion teachers' brief for this age group is to take advanced lessons in moral decision making. The teacher would offer some input with time included for questions and answers. Sometimes this session would take the form of class discussion but despite a set agenda on my part questions of a topical or controversial nature would arise. These have to be dealt with on the spot. One such class took place on a day after the media had been full of negative remarks about priesthood. It also quoted young people as saying that they had no interest in institutional religion. Yet, here was I in a class of twenty sixth years openly asking demanding and searching questions about the role of priesthood in Catholic Christianity.

My day in school would not necessarily always consist of the above structure. Sometimes I would spend it meeting students individually. I meet them in the chaplain's room beside the school oratory which is bright comfortable and welcoming. Alternatively, I would call into a class to prepare or celebrate a class Mass, take certain classes for retreat days, or just take half an hour walking around the school yard. At other times I would have a cup of tea with the staff or attend a sporting event. The one day a week I spend meeting the students is a big commitment for me and there were times when I felt it was time wasting. However, deep down I know this is not the case. It is only in this way that the chaplain can build up relationships in ministry. Am I wasting my time when I try to understand the world of teenagers, listen to their concerns, answer their questions and journey with them as they search for meaning? In a school that is geared towards examination and points, I focus my one-to-one meeting on the intrinsic value and worth of each person. I allow the students to ask the questions that might not be appropriate in class. Our time together allows them to raise questions about human identity and destiny, justice and society, faith and politics, science and religion, morality and literature, ecology and creation and biology and sexuality. This private level of sharing, in its turn, allows for opportunities to have serious open discussions when I take occasional classes.

School and parish

One of the advantages of being a curate assigned to a parish is that it complements my work as a school chaplain. Parish and school are supposed to complement one another! I see my work in the school as a very important extension of my parish ministry. Through contact with the students I have been able to involve them in the parish as faith-friends in the confirmation programme, as readers of the word and as Ministers of the Eucharist. Since I know my students I have been able to encourage some of them to make home visitations of the elderly and the infirm. They often enjoy doing the garden and other useful jobs for the older generation with whom they have made friends. Through these varied ministries, many of the students have become involved in parish life and are readily available when their support is needed.

Finally, the bottom line for me is not to fear that the gospel no longer has the power to attract human beings. I try to face the school and the world in which I live through the eyes of Christ. I want to bring the good news to others. While some of my students are openly indifferent to religion and are turning away from the church, they still believe in God. I would never force the message of the gospel upon them nor would I water it down simply to make it more acceptable for those who are not interested in it. The real challenge for me is to be authentic and to live the good news myself to the best of my ability. Young people are searching and part of that search is for meaning and God. As Paul VI once said:

> It is often said that our age is thirsting for sincerity and honesty. Young people in particular are said to have a horror of falsity and hypocrisy and seek above all truth and clarity. The world, in spite of the general opinion to the contrary, and although it gives every outward sign of denying God, is in fact seeking God by strange ways and is in desperate need of God.

Reflections of a Religious Sister
Ann O'Donoghue

In the evening when I return home from school, I often wonder what I have been doing with my time. I know that I have been on my feet constantly and that each day is different from the previous one. Life on the corridors of the school is not the same as life in the classroom where I once taught. As chaplain, one becomes involved in almost every aspect of school life, perhaps even too involved at times. Some of the activities I would have carried out during the year are as follows:

- meeting students on an individual basis.
- meeting staff members on an individual basis.
- visiting religious education classes.
- organising liturgies.
- sitting with staff members having a social chat.
- visiting homes.
- inviting parents to the school and also helping them through some of their own difficulties.
- meeting with the religious education team/pastoral care team, career guidance teachers, year heads, tutors, principal/vice-principal.
- spending time on the corridors talking to students.
- returning sick students to their homes.
- visiting students who are in hospital.

The faith dimension

Church attendance in our parish is not high – the reality is that very few of our students return to church on Sundays after they receive the sacrament of confirmation. Many of their parents do not attend church either. In this locality the truth is that the sacraments are not perceived as high points either in the lives of the parents or their children. Yet, my experience in school with the students points to a belief in God that is very strong. Not all students, of course, are Catholic as there are quite a number in the school who are Buddhists, Muslims, The Church of God, Baptists, Jehovah Witnesses and Church of Ireland. Yet, like Catholic students, it appears that very few practice. regardless of the denomination. Many wandered into my office last year at different times asking for prayers, medals or holy water. Sometimes the need for these sacramentals sprung from a tragedy in the local community such as a suicide, a fatal accident or a murder. Interestingly, it is often the grandparents who teach the children the benefits and blessings of the tangible symbol. Also at times like these the students will want to pray in our oratory, practice some form of religious expression and speak openly about their belief in God.

Meeting students on a one-to-one basis

A great need exists for individual contact with students. While they are often referred to the chaplain by members of staff, many have found their own way to my office. I have also trained as a counsellor which is particularly useful when dealing with people on a one-to-one situation. Many of the students require a 'significant adult' in their lives for a given period of time. It is my firm belief that the chaplain can be that person through encouragement, building self esteem, listening, caring, challenging, helping students to make choices and teaching about value systems and forgiveness. Ours is an increasingly complex world in which a young person finds it difficult to learn about him/herself. As chaplain I know that I have helped young adolescents to tackle some specific aspects of their lives that warranted attention. Sometimes, however, I feel that my hands are tied, that there is very little I can do except simply to listen. I have learned that I cannot do everything, that I do not have all the answers. Most of the time I am 'just there' for the student who needs support.

My purpose as chaplain

Jean Vanier, in his book *The Body Broken – Journey to Wholeness,* encapsulates an important aspect of the role of chaplaincy when he suggests that:

> *It is important to approach people in their brokenness and littleness gently, so gently, not forcing yourself upon them, but accepting them as they are, with humility and respect.*

In this way I have learned to befriend a school community by engaging in the struggles, hopes and pains of all those with whom I come in contact throughout my working day. I have tried to listen and to understand. Within that context my sense of purpose is strong, which is, to bring people a little closer to Jesus Christ who binds up all wounds and brings peace.

Reflections of a Primary School Chaplain

Alex Conlan

When I was asked to write this article I hesitated somewhat, wondering where to begin writing about a part of my priestly life that I have always taken for granted. The role of school chaplain has, for me, been the hub of my pastoral ministry.

Mighty long time

The words of a song come to mind, 'Twenty one years is a mighty long time'. Yes, in that length of ministry in the Dublin diocese I have had a varied experience of schools. These have included a tiny rural school, large suburban and urban schools, schools with hundreds of boys and mixed schools with hundreds of boys and girls. Despite the variety, the basic lesson to be learned is that although their social, religious or other needs may vary, children are the same everywhere.

Christ in his ministry had a special place for children. Scripture reminds us of our responsibility towards children, 'Anyone who welcomes this little child in my name welcomes me; and anyone who welcomes me welcomes the one who sent me. For the least among you all, that is the one who is great' (Lk 9:48). This is why it is sad to hear of schools who seldom see their priest. My response has always been 'where are they?' No, they are not always weighed down by other pastoral duties. In my years I have been criticised for spending too much time in schools. I will let the pupils, parents and teachers be my judge.

So much of a priest's pastoral duties in a parish can be complemented by regular school visitation. 'How often?', one might ask. 'Every day' is the answer, or at least almost everyday. The length of the visit is not as important as the frequency. While many may lament the unavailability of priests for the traditional house-to-house visitation, it is surprising how that part of the ministry can be substituted to some extent by school chaplaincy. The child is the entrance to every home. Remember the first contact many couples have with the church today is through children for baptism, first communion and confirmation. While your face may not be known in a home, your name can be a familiar one. Parents have always very much appreciated my involvement with their children. On house visitation it is encouraging to be greeted by a parent with, 'I've heard so much about you', or by a child, 'that's my priest'.

A Game of Conkers

Chaplaincy is not confined to classroom contact. My experiences have proven to me that 'yard' contact is also very important. In the yard children have the freedom to talk with a priest at another and less formal level. It is important to befriend children so that they can see you on their level. Yard contact might involve taking part in a game of 'conkers' or turning the rope for skipping. It might also involve tying laces, consoling the wounded, hearing about the birthday, the new baby, the sick granny or pet, leaving the wiping of noses to the teacher on yard duty. (It is important, however, not to take from the responsibility of the teacher who is on yard duty.) We all like to be addressed by name and children are no different. It means a lot to children when the priest knows their name. Yard contact is an ideal opportunity to develop this technique. The ability to remember names does, of course, vary from person to person.

Sacramental preparation can form a large part of a chaplain's duties. One must, however, take care not to neglect contact with other classes in the process. Informal discussions with classes on what they are covering with their teacher should be done in a way that does not query the teacher's coverage of the religion programme. Teachers have always appreciated my input and visitation and this encourages a priest in his ministry. The seasons of the church's year, feasts, saints, Our Lady, the sacraments, commandments and the gospel stories, give great scope and variety for classroom contact.

Children love handouts. Bring pictures with gospel illustrations that require colouring and let the children keep them. This is always a big hit, especially with younger children. Holy pictures and medals are also among the much appreciated handouts offered to children. A time for questions, even the ones we sometimes cannot answer, is also very important. Frequent short visits are more effective than infrequent longer ones. Regular weekly contact with classes before the reception of sacraments is of vital importance.

Class Masses are an opportunity to bring children closer to Christ and they help them to participate in a more meaningful way in the community celebration on Sunday. Although general participation in the liturgy should be encouraged by parents, teachers and priests, this is sometimes hindered by parish personnel who do not recognise the importance of the child in the celebration of liturgies. Meaningful offertory processions for liturgical seasons are of great relevance to children. For example, the presentation of Easter and Christmas by way of play or mime serves to bring these mysteries to life.

The role of the school chaplain is to complement the work of teachers in the classroom in handing on the faith. It is also complementary to parents who are the first teachers of their children in the ways of faith. In today's sometimes Godless world, though, some children's only contact with the church is the priest in the school. Children, in their turn, very often are the ones who bring parents to Mass rather than the other way around. Reminiscent of two thousand years ago, one exceptional adult said:

Let the little children come to me, and do not stop them; for it is to such as these that the kingdom of God belongs. I tell you solemnly, anyone who does not welcome the kingdom of God like a little child will never enter it (Lk 18:15-17).

Reflections of a parent
Pauline King

Enter the chaplain! Who is this person? What role is played by the chaplain in the school community? Is there a necessity for this person? Is a chaplain, lay or religious, likely to force 'religion' down the throats of our young people? What will the chaplain do for my child? Perhaps the chaplain has nothing to do with us anyway?

Your life as parents begins with a little bundle of joy. As the first few years progress from babyhood to early childhood, this tiny infant depends on you totally. The process is one of learning, growing and developing in an interactive way which affects both child and parent. In the blink of an eye the first five years fly by and primary school beckons. Even if your child has attended nursery school, there is a tangible change between that and the child's formal education.

The school years

At primary level the change in your child becomes keenly apparent. All you seem to hear from your 'baby' is 'teacher says this' and 'teacher says that'. Suddenly you realise that your are sharing your child with someone else, someone who is also special to the child. Nonetheless, you have to let go and that can be hard. You must remember that this is a time of adventure and development for the child which demands adjustment on your part.

After the quickest eight years of parent/teacher meetings, sales of work, school trips, plays, sports days, first communion and, finally, the 'big one', confirmation, you feel prepared for the next step – second level education, another chapter in all your lives. Yet, maybe you are not as ready as you thought. Instead of having just one teacher your child now has seven or eight excluding the guidance counsellor, remedial teacher and, if fortunate enough, the chaplain. Here you have people who are specialists in an array of subjects all mapping out *your* child's future. However, while all of these people claim a significant role in the life of your child, the chaplain is the one who might well have the most crucial part to play.

The chaplain

For example, the chaplain would have a greater awareness that some teenagers question the need for God in their lives. Many would seriously question institutionalised religion, finding it irrelevant and the liturgical practice of it boring. Religious parents often find their offspring rebelling against church teaching and authority, even to the point of finding attendance at Mass embarrassing because it is something that 'oldies' do. In this context, how many parents can identify with the favourite modern teenage dictum, 'it's a waste of space'? Where the good chaplain comes in is to meet the young people on their terms. From a position of greater independence and objectivity, the chaplain is sometimes better able to provide the religious guidelines required for a life of faith. This can be very enlightening for the teenager. Yet, while pupils may get used to seeing the chaplain around on a regular basis, the parents, living and working in a different environment, are less likely to be aware of the everyday role of the chaplain.

So what part might the chaplain play at this significant stage of life for both parents and students? Perhaps the most important thing is for the chaplain to encourage parents to take a further look at their own development. It might be possible for the chaplain to assist the parents in the discovery of their own hidden, inner abilities. In certain cases, sometimes at an early age, the talents of many parents were set aside or suppressed owing to the demands of parenthood. As a result many parents suffered from a lack of self-esteem. Where this has been neglected, they might now have the time and inclination to pay greater attention to their personal, social and educational needs. It may even be possible that the chaplain might be the one to harness the energy of these considerations to the good of the parents and the wider school community.

Accordingly, the chaplain might set up a Parents Resource Group. In time it would be possible for this group to run courses and programmes to suit the needs of other parents. For example, work done in areas such as drugs, peer pressure, bullying, personal awareness, assistance to teachers, bereavement, separation and home study timetabling, might accomplish great results. If parents were to be recruited annually to the resource group it would give the necessary injection of new ideas and energy. The success of the group would depend on the enthusiasm and interest of the chaplain, with the added advantage of leaving the chaplain free to explore fresh avenues of development for the future.

What is most encouraging for parents is that, in a society which places a great deal of pressure on young people, the chaplain is a sensitive, caring, reliable and available resource for all connected with second level schooling. Where the chaplain works together with the parents, it is possible that our teenagers will emerge well adjusted after five or six years of the school cycle. This working together will contribute to the self-esteem and confidence of the young people. In turn they will become persons who will be capable of giving to, rather than taking from, society. I read once of the parent-child relationship that, 'our children are like arrows and we are the bows'. It is up to the parents to send the 'arrows' out into the world in good condition. Undoubtedly, it is up to the chaplain to remember that the 'bows' also need tending.

Reflections of a Community School Chaplain

James Norman

The chaplain is the person who is always around the school corridors with a smile, the one who gives students a lift in the car, the one who leaves you with an abiding impression of presence and meeting your needs. The concept of the kind and friendly chaplain should remain constant. The school chaplain might organise excellent liturgies, faith development programmes, home visitation and much more besides. But, the measure of our work lies in the experience of our young people and how they perceive us.

Availability and care depend on the chaplain's own willingness to imitate Jesus. As Jesus did not build up the reign of God in isolation, neither should the chaplain. The chaplain's work, therefore, has to take place within the context of partnership which includes staff, students, parents and parishioners. When I was posted to Killinarden Community School, I learned that a group of parishioners were already involved in the life of the school. These willing people had already been trained to run specific programmes with the students. It was clear that this group had great potential to become a chaplaincy team. Setting up the team was not going to be easy for a number of reasons. Firstly, the running of any school is always organised strictly on a timetabled basis. When I needed to collaborate with staff or students, I was free but they were not. Making appointments takes time and patience.

Secondly, school staff are not always aware of the role of the chaplain or the significance attaching to it. It was necessary, therefore, to convince the staff that the chaplain plays a key part in the life of the school. Very often the perception of chaplaincy is circumscribed by the teachers' own experience of teaching. Questions about how many hours the chaplain is expected to teach or what exactly the chaplain is supposed to do, reveals a lack of understanding of the need for chaplaincy in a community school. This is because teaching is defined by the curriculum whereas chaplaincy is defined by the faith and person of the chaplain. Generally, the ability to communicate that faith to others is less easy to convey than the content matter of a given subject.

Confidence building

Keeping in mind the aspirations of the Second Vatican Council, *all* the People of God should be encouraged to take part in the building up of the church. Unfortunately, this has not always been the case. Yet, in Killinarden the opportunity had already presented itself particularly with the group of parishioners who had been trained to work with the students on certain projects. Building confidence is where it begins. This selfless group were invited to become a team who would work *with* the chaplain rather than *for* the chaplain. At first, all forms of persuasion were tried ranging anywhere between subtle suggestions and avid challenges. The greater the responsibility given to those involved in the chaplaincy team, the greater the confidence was gained. It was a continual process which encouraged them to take initiatives and make decisions normally not expected of them. Sometimes this process was a difficult one, as they were asked to find retreat teams and venues where the outcome might not always be successful. However, as each new decision was taken the individuals became ever more aware of their new role as members of the newly formed autonomous team.

The use of language

A significant part of the building up of the chaplaincy team is to be aware of the use of language. The *helpers,* for example, became the *team* with the latter term appearing on all subsequent correspondence both within and outwith the school environment. The language of team is different from the language of the individual. *I* becomes *we* and the implications of this shift in perception are as challenging as they are rewarding. Taking part in collaborative ministry involves a process rather than a single event. The chaplain, in particular, should not run with an idea that has not been discussed in consultation with the rest of the team. Nobody would ever consider producing a school play without scriptwriters, actors and directors. Yet, some chaplains will often organise a major school liturgy without any other person having been involved in the preparation of it.

Slower is often better

It is slower but more effective to call a team meeting when planning a retreat, a prayer service or a project. Nonetheless, my own perception of myself as a team member develops each time the team meets, prays, plans and puts work into effect. When an individual has an idea and brings it to the team, it is torn apart and remoulded until something better takes shape. It then becomes something the whole team can own.

Maturity and trust

It may seem patronising to say that a school chaplain should be mature. However, the type of maturity needed to be a member of a collaborative team is very specific. Each member of the team has to be confident about the gifts and realistic about the limitations he or she has to offer. Having the ability to trust in the opinion and actions of another, requires a maturity rooted in respectful and honest relationships. This will only come about if the team has a strong foundation. An annual retreat for the chaplaincy team is well worthwhile. Here we are given the opportunity to pray and reflect on our own lives and ministry together. Some members of the team may even be available on a weekly basis to read and to reflect upon the forthcoming Sunday's gospel. Its relevance to our personal lives will shape and enhance our ministry in the school. A chaplaincy team which is rooted in prayer and training will thrive on a relationship of trust.

Publicity

Finally, if the chaplaincy team is to make a statement about itself and its aims, some kind of publicity about their respective roles in the school community is essential. Putting together a brochure about the team provides such an opportunity. A brochure will raise the profile of the work of the chaplaincy team, ultimately benefitting those to whom we minister. Indeed, the preparation of the brochure is in itself a collaborative exercise since it requires planning in order to tell others about who we are and what we do. *(See chapter 9, Resource Ideas: A Sample Brochure.)*

Reflections of a Catechist
Robert Dunne

Schools are complex organisations. Every problem in society influences the life of the school. Aware of this reality, many schools have now in place structures to assist in the emotional growth of their students. Whereas in the past pastoral care was seen as the responsibility of the religious education teacher and the chaplain, it is now viewed as a whole school issue. The principal, vice principal, guidance counsellor, year heads, tutors home-school liaison teacher, general staff, all work together to ensure that the school is experienced as a caring and compassionate Christian community. The chaplain is a professional working with professionals and, as such, brings an expertise to the school. School chaplaincy is specialised work which demands a familiarity with basic counselling skills, adolescent psychology, a basic knowledge of the theory and practice of religious education and, most importantly, a creative approach to school liturgy. The need to equip chaplains with such skills is acknowledged with the formation of specific courses for school chaplains. School chaplaincy is no longer a position to drift into; it is a specialised cog of the pastoral wheel of the school.

Titles fail to impress teenagers. They have high standards for those of us who present a vision of life that, for many, seems to be but an ideal. The person behind the post of chaplain gives the post credibility and respectability. They expect us to be authentic. We must be ourselves and be committed to the value system that we preach. Hypocrisy is spurned but an admission of failure is understood, not judged. Teenagers appreciate our experience and enjoy listening to the stories of that experience. They respect those who are open to the human encounter, those who are kind, and most of all those who listen. Often the adult in school is the only adult in their world who listens to them. Acceptance of their ideas is not expected but direct criticism can be difficult to take. It is best to move the student gently in a more purposeful direction. The effective chaplain works out of a theology of friendship.

Strong friendships

Strong friendships demand time. Many who find themselves in the position of chaplain may also have demanding roles in parishes and may find that time is limited. Time spent in school, however, is time well spent. A chaplain cannot function effectively by staying in an office but must be wherever students situate themselves. In reality, this implies chatting in corridors, attending assemblies, shivering on the sidelines supporting the school teams, climbing mountains, hostelling and generally being available. When you are around students, it is then that you notice the withdrawn student, the sad student, the student who needs, at that moment, the smile or the supportive word. But perhaps more importantly, when you are around students, it is then that they notice you and, therefore, when in difficulty might seek you out to chat over their problems.

Every human difficulty is experienced in a school and a chaplain in the counselling situation is called to be a true disciple as he/she walks with a student on this rocky section of the path of life. It is during the experience of the shadow side of life that key questions are raised for the teenager such as, 'where do I come from?', 'where am I going?', 'why pain, suffering and death?' The chaplain can play a significant role in addressing these difficulties. Some of the most graced moments in our school have been experienced during services organised in response to tragedy. At these times the curriculum has no words to meet the occasion. Students find peace in gathering. The ritual is healing. Eli Wiesel's comment that no one can fight the night alone and hope to conquer it, aptly describes the importance of facilitating such a communal response for students. The chaplain just needs to be present at these times. Words are not necessary when explanations are impossible.

Spirituality

While many teenagers have difficulty with organised religion, they recognise their need for God. They have a spirituality. Spirituality, in the words of Cardinal Hume, is the process of getting to know how to love God. Spirituality is the soul of religion. Students want to pray. Students often demand to pray. Many catechists will testify to classes requesting to meditate. Prayer rooms are seen as an oasis of peace amidst a world of noise and toil. The chaplain is in the privileged position to guide students and to explore various prayer methods which bring peace and fulfilment. These are insights that are more valuable and will remain with the students longer than those gleaned from some of the purely academic subjects.

For many, school is the only positive experience of Christian community. While acknowledging the many fine initiatives taking place at parish level, the point of contact with teenagers seems to be difficult to make. It is essential, then, to ensure that every liturgical celebration in school is a special celebration. The liturgical year provides the chaplain with opportunities to highlight the liturgical seasons. It is important to grasp opportunities from the secular world and point out their religious significance. For example, 'Mothers' Day' and 'One World Week', to name but two. Advent and Lent offer times to celebrate the sacrament of Reconciliation. Communication is necessary between catechists and the chaplain if the most is to be made of these opportunities. Preparatory work completed in class will add to the actual liturgical celebration of the sacraments.

The encouraging word

The chaplain is one of the few people on the staff who can be the same with staff and students. Most of the staff portray different *personae* in the classroom. The staff are carers in the school and as such are often people in need of care and support themselves. The chaplain can encourage and help the staff. The encouraging word and the supportive smile can do as much for the staff as for the students. It is essential, however, that the chaplain takes care of his/her own needs also. It is important for anyone in ministry to have a support network of friends, to be part of a professional group such as the Chaplains' Association and to engage in hobbies that can relax and replenish energy. Only then is the chaplain in a position to help the school community effectively.

The work of the chaplain, like the work of the catechist, is personally challenging. In both roles we rarely see the results of our efforts. It can be easy to become disillusioned when one rarely meets with success but faces failure often. The gospel of the Sower has much to offer us. We plant the seed but only in years to come does it bear fruit. Yes, the demands are many. The work is hard. But, we must trust that the hand of God is to be found in our encounters. Our work is valuable. We make a difference.

Further Resources and Reading.

What follows is merely a taste of what is available.

A. Practical Resource Guides

Forty Masses with Young People. Donal Neary. (Columba Press, Dublin, 1985) A very good resource for chaplains and catechists.

Sadhana - A Way to God. Anthony de Mello. (Anand, India, 1978) One of many excellent guides to meditation by de Mello. His publications offer many suggestions, stories in the area of prayer and faith. There are also videos and tapes to supplement his books.

Reflecting – Complete Assemblies for Secondary Schools. Jan Thompson. (Hodder & Staughton, Kent, England, 1988) Many ideas, prayer texts and stories to use and adapt.

Worship Dramas for Children and Adults. Cathy Lee & Chris Uhlmann. (Resource Publications, San Jose, USA, 1988) Very worthwhile suggestions for the primary sector in particular.

Youth Ministry Activity Book. Rose Thomas Stupak. (Resource Publications, San Jose, USA) Good ideas for primary schools – games, faith projects, discussion starters.

New Gatherings. Bronwen Wild. (Hodder & Stoughton, Kent, England, 1992) Readings, stories, reflections for assemblies and prayer services.

Creative Resources for Youth Ministry. Yvette Nelson (ed). (St Mary's Press, Minnesota, USA, 1991) A source of ideas in working with a small group of youth interested in faith development.

Faith Works. Lisa M. Calderone-Stewart. (St Mary's Press, Minnesota, USA, 1993) Useful in working with a group wishing to deepen their faith.

Love Needs Learning. Margaret Vincent. (Geoffrey Chapman, London, 1994) An excellent resource for a relationships course with senior post-primary students.

Faith Questions. Francis McCrickard. (Veritas, Dublin, 1989) A resource in working with small groups in the area of faith development.

Break-Through. Disability Awareness for Young People. Michael Shevlin /Patricia Noonan Walsh. (St Michael's House Research, Dublin, 1994) A well put together series of class plans to deal with this important area.

Building Self-Esteem – A Workbook for Teens. Jerome Trahey. (Resource Publications, San Jose, 1992) A very helpful resource from the Christian perspective.

Resources for Catechists and Chaplains. Margaret McEntee. (Columba Press, Dublin, 1994) A vast array of resources to use in many different circumstances.

Create Community With Christ. Robert Doolittle. (St Mary's Press, Minnesota, 1991) A collection of youth group strategies. There is a companion volume entitled, *Be Alive Christ.*

It's Not Fair. (A Christian Aid Publication 1993) An excellent resource on world development issues.

Living with Death. Judith Bisignano. (Good Apple, Illinois, USA, 1991) One in a series of workbooks exploring issues such as stress, relationships and personal development. Particularly suitable for the primary context.

Youth Retreats. Aileen Doyle. (St Mary's Press, Minnesota, USA, 1986) One of the many resources available to assist in putting a school/parish retreat together for young people.

Yes, You Do Count. Maura Ward. (The Church's Peace Education Programme, 1995) This is a comprehensive programme for senior students.

B. Background Reading

Changing Children. Paul Andrews. (Gill & Macmillan, Dublin, 1994) A good insight into the young person of today – their concerns, their needs, their pressures.

Adolescent Spirituality. Charles Shelton. (Loyola University Press, Chicago, 1983) A basic text in understanding the adolescent – of enduring relevance.

Wasting Time in Schools. Mary McKeone. (St Paul's, Slough, England, 1993) A wonderful personal story of chaplaincy – thought provoking, entertaining and resourceful.

Chaplaincy: The Change and the Challenge. (Association of Catholic Chaplains in Education, England. 1996) A fine document seeking to outline the role of the chaplain in the contemporary school.

Life to the Full: A Vision of Catholic Education. (Northern Ireland Council of Catholic Maintained Schools. 1996) A well put together overview of the distinctive elements of the Catholic School.

Schools of Reconciliation. Priscilla Chadwick. (Cassell, London, 1994) An investigation of some important ecumenical questions.

The Contemporary Catholic School. Terence McLaughlin et al (eds.) (Falmer Press, London 1996) A comprehensive study of this theme.

Pastoral Care and Personal-Social Education. Ron Best et al (eds). (Cassell, London, 1995) An excellent guide to these developing areas of school life. Addresses issues such as working with individuals, dealing with traumas and the home-school link.

Making School a Better Place. Luke Monahan. (Marino Institute of Education, Dublin, 1996) An exploration of pastoral care as a value-laden approach to life in the school community.

The Class Tutor: The Why... The What The How. Luke Monahan. (Irish Association of Pastoral Care in Education, Dublin, 1997) A detailed investigation of this key pastoral role in the school – one with which the chaplain will often be in relationship.

Pastoral Care Matters in Primary and Middle Schools. Kenneth David & Tony Charlton (eds). (Routledge, London, 1996) A range of issues in the pastoral care field are addressed.

School 2000. Jim Lyons. (Clare Education Centre, Ireland, 1997) This work explores the relationships which constitute good schools.

Contributors

LUKE MONAHAN S.M. is a Marist priest, chaplain to Chanel College Coolock and lecturer in Marino Institute of Education, Dublin.

ELIZABETH COTTER is a Loreto sister and principal of Loreto College, St Stephen's Green, Dublin.

DAVID KAVANAGH is a lay chaplain to Balally Community School, Dublin.

JOHN KELLY is a curate in Donnycarney parish and chaplain to Ard Scoil Rís Secondary CBS school, Dublin.

ANN O'DONOGHUE is a Loreto sister, a catechist, counsellor and chaplain to St. Aidan's Community School, Tallaght, Dublin.

ALEX CONLAN is curate in the parish of Avoca Templerainey, Co Wicklow. He is also chaplain to St Joseph's National School Templerainey, St John's National School, Redcross, and Arklow Community College.

PAULINE KING is a mother of three children and a member of Chanel College Parents' Council, Coolock, Dublin.

JAMES NORMAN is a priest and chaplain to Killinarden Community School, Tallaght, Dublin.

ROBERT DUNNE is a catechist and history teacher in Loreto College, Dalkey and he tutors in educational methodologies in Mater Dei Institute, Dublin.

MICHAEL MARTIN, OFM is head of chaplaincy services in the Dublin Institute of Technology. He is a Franciscan friar and a poet.

RUTH O'ROURKE has just completed a Masters degree in the area of Death Education at Trinity College, Dublin. She is a counsellor and a teacher in Margaret Aylward Community College, Whitehall, Dublin.

CAROLINE RENEHAN is a Post-Primary Adviser for the Archdiocese of Dublin. She also lectures in theology in Mater Dei Institute, Dublin, and in Religious Education in University College, Dublin.